WE HAVE OBSERVED A SHIFT IN HOW PEOPLE LIVE AND WORK. AMERICANS ARE BEGINNING TO LIVE AND WORK AS ARTISTS AND SCIENTISTS ALWAYS HAVE, AND THEY ARE MAKING LIVING AND WORKPLACE CHOICES THAT FACILITATE CREATIVE LIFESTYLES.

SHUBIN + DONALDSON

LIVE + WORK

MODERN HOMES AND OFFICES

THE SOUTHERN CALIFORNIA ARCHITECTURE OF SHUBIN + DONALDSON

ESSAYS BY THOM MAYNE
AND JOSEPH GIOVANNINI

ORO *editions*
Publishers of Architecture, Art, Design and Photography
Gordon Goff - Publisher
USA: PO Box 998, Pt Reyes Station, CA 94956
Asia: Block 8, Lorong Bakar Batu #02-04 Singapore 348743
www.oroeditions.com
info@oroeditions.com

ISBN: 978-0-9795395-5-8

Production and Project Coordination: Joanne Tan and Davina Tjandra
Color Separation and Printing: ORO *Group Ltd*

ORO *editions* has made every effort to minimize the carbon footprint of this project. In pursuit of this goal, ORO *editions*, in association with Global ReLeaf, has arranged to plant two trees for each and every tree used in the manufacturing of the FSC paper produced for this book. Global ReLeaf is an international campaign run by American Forests, the nation's oldest nonprofit conservation organization. Global ReLeaf is American Forests' education and action program that helps individuals, organizations, agencies, and corporations improve the local and global environment by planting and caring for trees.

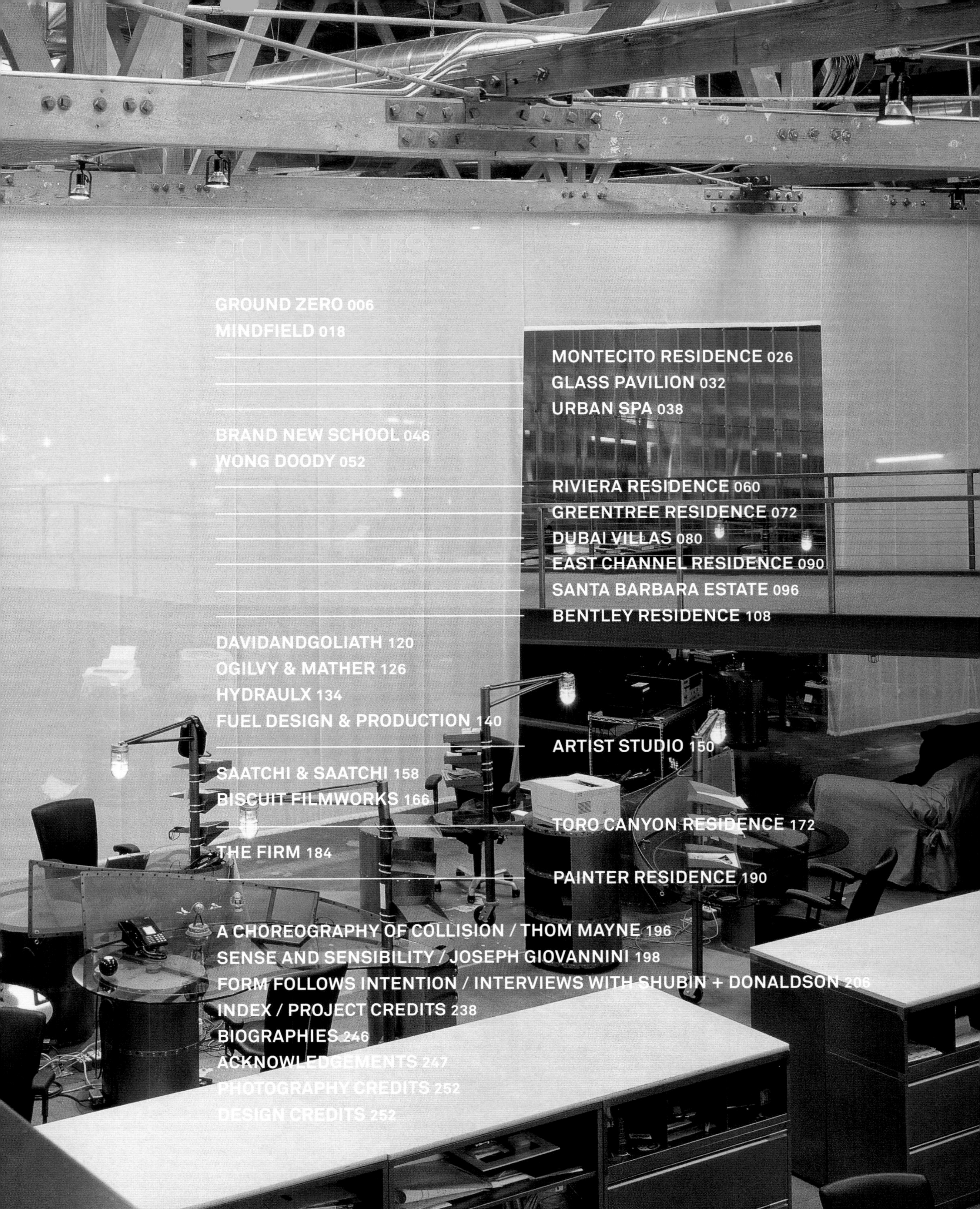

CONTENTS

GROUND ZERO 006
MINDFIELD 018
MONTECITO RESIDENCE 026
GLASS PAVILION 032
URBAN SPA 038
BRAND NEW SCHOOL 046
WONG DOODY 052
RIVIERA RESIDENCE 060
GREENTREE RESIDENCE 072
DUBAI VILLAS 080
EAST CHANNEL RESIDENCE 090
SANTA BARBARA ESTATE 096
BENTLEY RESIDENCE 108
DAVIDANDGOLIATH 120
OGILVY & MATHER 126
HYDRAULX 134
FUEL DESIGN & PRODUCTION 140
ARTIST STUDIO 150
SAATCHI & SAATCHI 158
BISCUIT FILMWORKS 166
TORO CANYON RESIDENCE 172
THE FIRM 184
PAINTER RESIDENCE 190
A CHOREOGRAPHY OF COLLISION / THOM MAYNE 196
SENSE AND SENSIBILITY / JOSEPH GIOVANNINI 198
FORM FOLLOWS INTENTION / INTERVIEWS WITH SHUBIN + DONALDSON 206
INDEX / PROJECT CREDITS 238
BIOGRAPHIES 246
ACKNOWLEDGEMENTS 247
PHOTOGRAPHY CREDITS 252
DESIGN CREDITS 252

GROUND ZERO
ADVERTISING AGENCY
MARINA DEL REY, CA / 1999

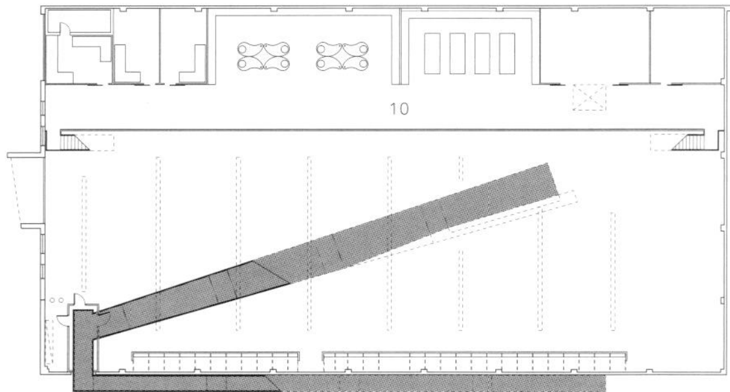

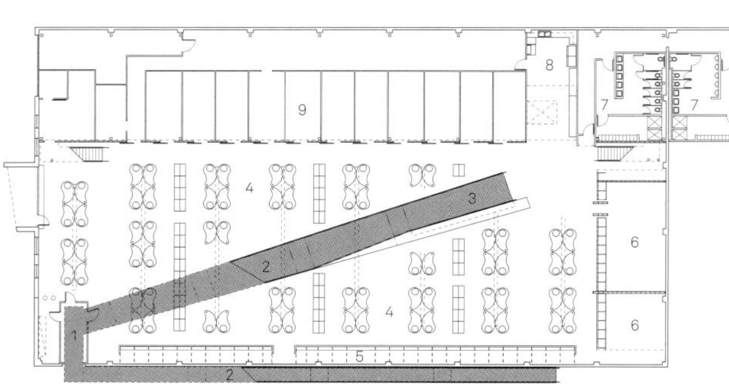

1 ENTRY
2 RAMP
3 RECEPTION
4 WORK STATIONS
5 STORAGE
6 CONFERENCE
7 RESTROOMS
8 KITCHEN
9 WAR ROOMS
10 MEZZANINE

MINDFIELD
POST-PRODUCTION
MARINA DEL REY, CA / 2000

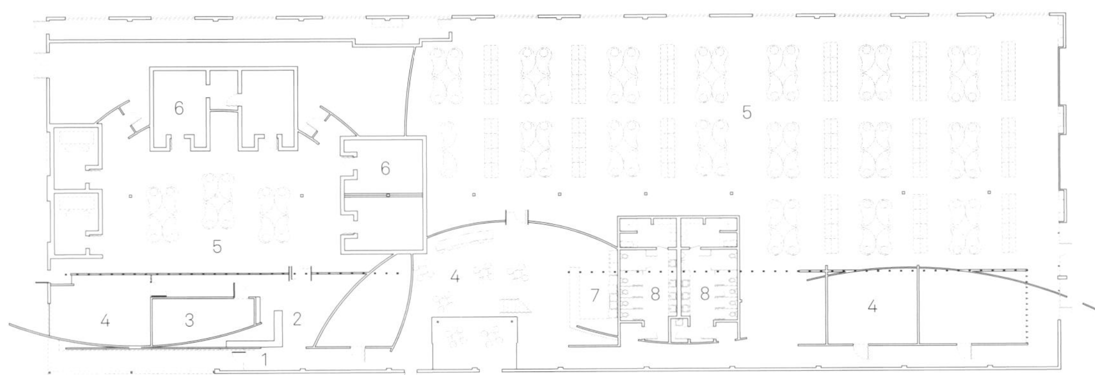

1 ENTRY
2 RECEPTION
3 OFFICE
4 CONFERENCE
5 OPEN WORK AREA
6 VIDEO EDITING
7 KITCHEN
8 RESTROOMS

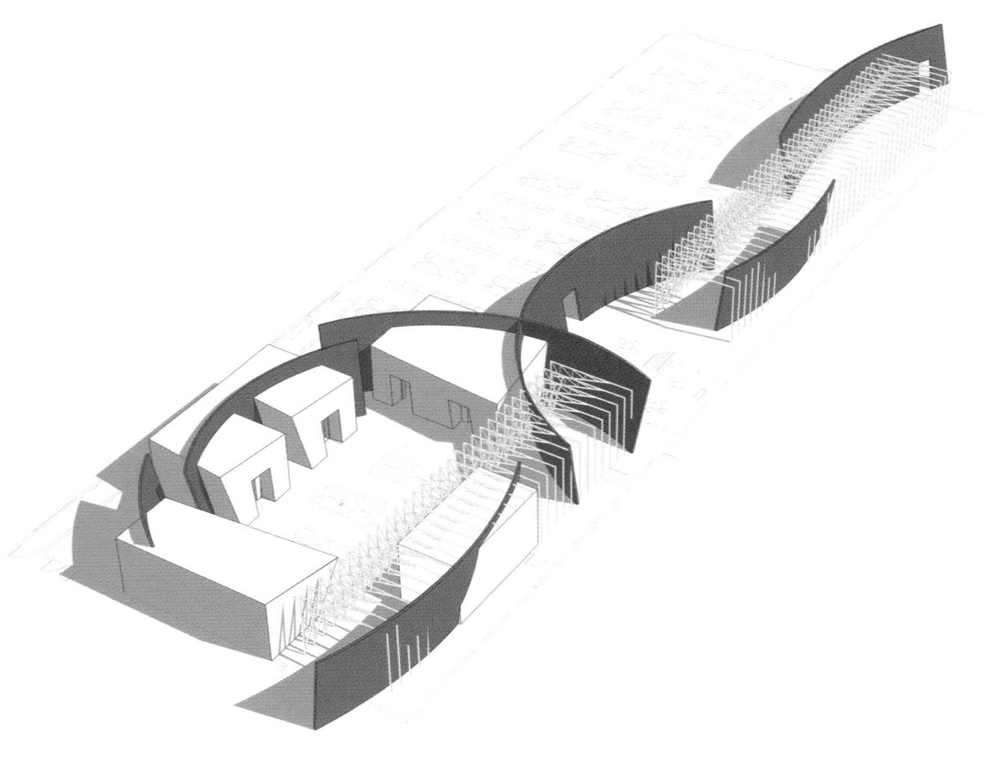

EXIT

MONTECITO RESIDENCE
MONTECITO, CA / 2000

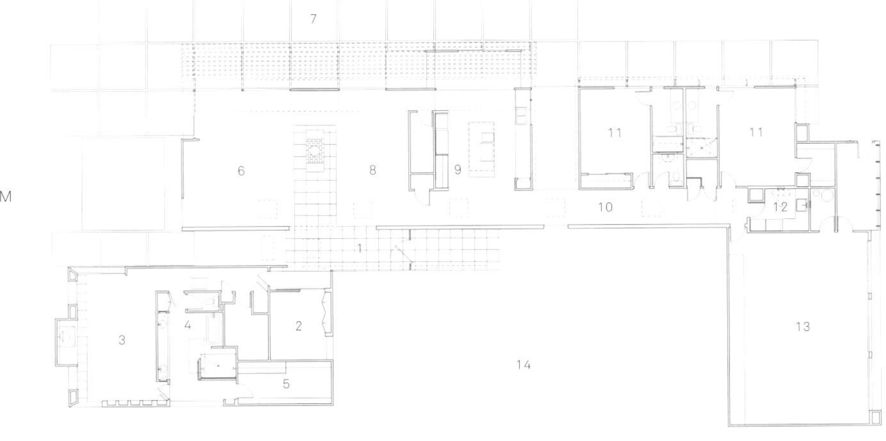

1 ENTRY
2 OFFICE
3 MASTER BEDROOM
4 MASTER BATH
5 CLOSET
6 LIVING
7 TERRACE / PATIO
8 DINING
9 KITCHEN
10 GALLERY
11 BEDROOM
12 LAUNDRY
13 GARAGE
14 MOTORCOURT

GLASS PAVILION
SANTA BARBARA, CA / 2006

1 GUEST STUDIO
2 BATH
3 GARAGE
4 ADDITION

SOUTH

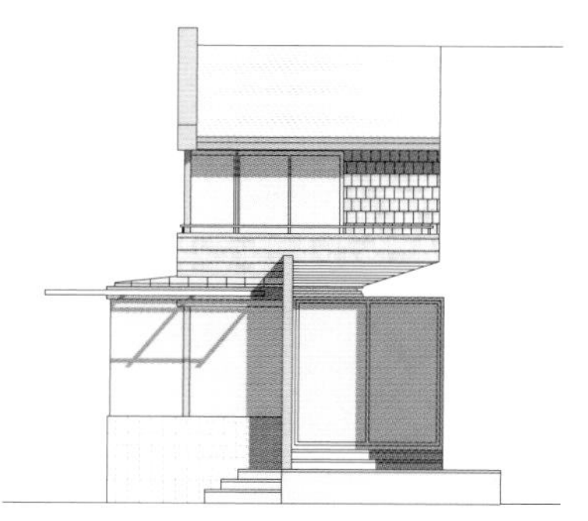

EAST

URBAN SPA
MALIBU, CA / 2002

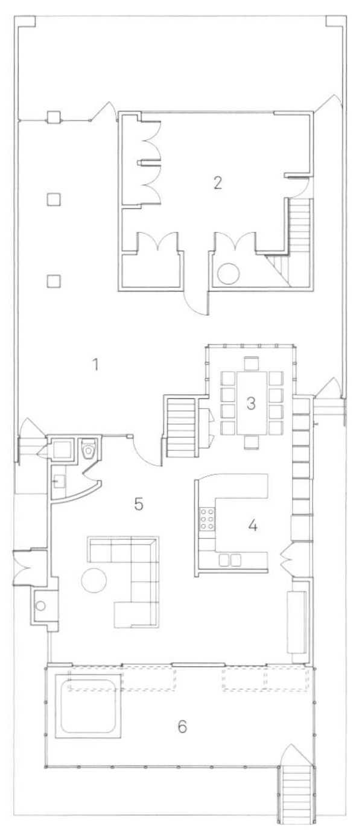
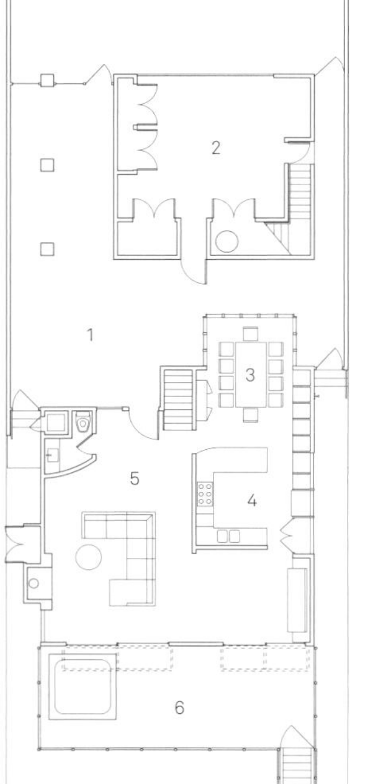

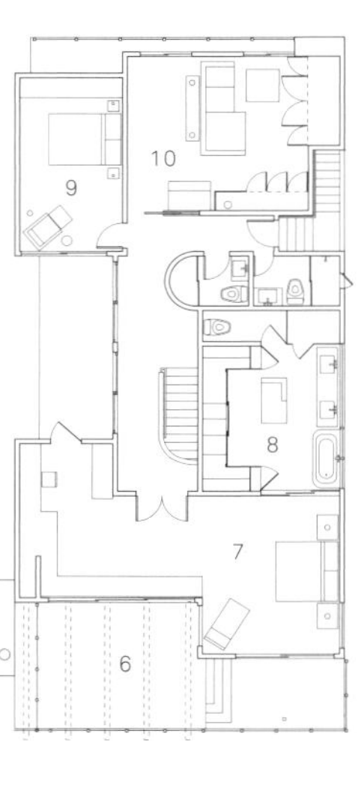

FIRST FLOOR

1 ENTRY COURT
2 GARAGE
3 DINING
4 KITCHEN
5 LIVING
6 DECK

SECOND FLOOR

7 MASTER BEDROOM
8 MASTER BATH
9 BEDROOM
10 MEDIA

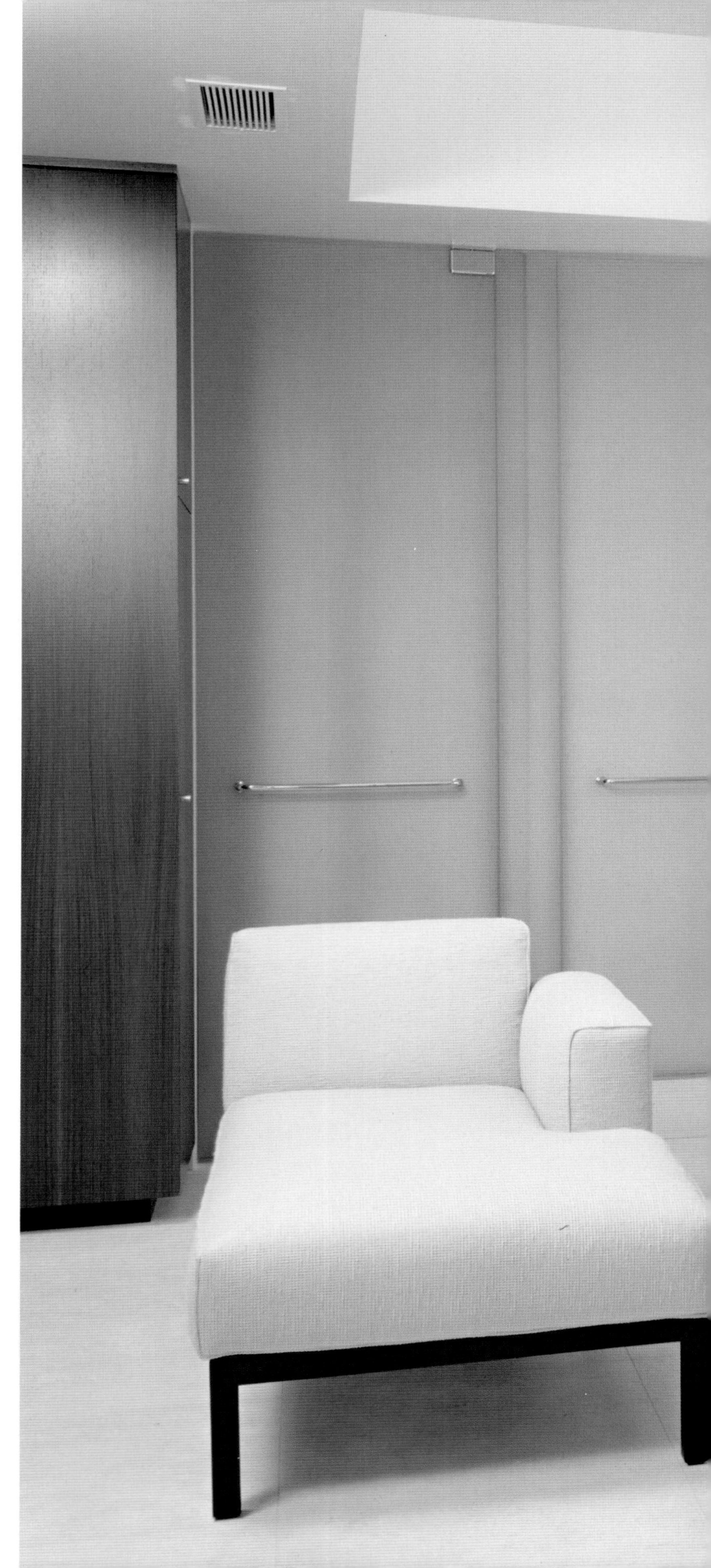

BRAND NEW SCHOOL

MOTION GRAPHICS
SANTA MONICA, CA / 2005

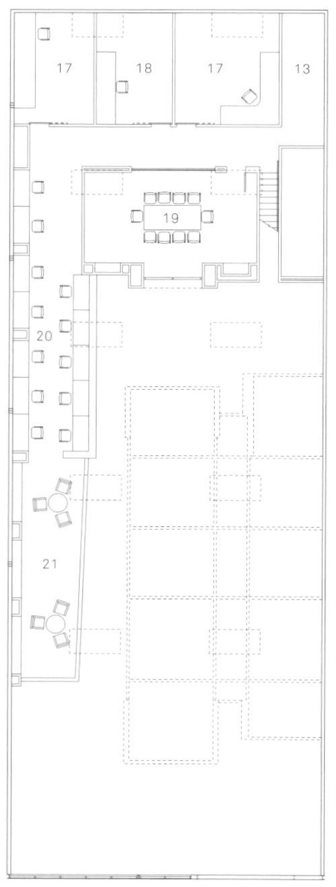

MEZZANINE

FIRST FLOOR

1 ENTRY
2 RECEPTION
3 LOBBY LOUNGE
4 PHOTO STAGING AREA
5 PRODUCERS OFFICES
6 COLLABORATIVE OFFICES
7 CREATIVE OFFICES
8 KITCHEN/BREAK AREA
9 COPY/MAIL
10 FINANCE
11 BOOK KEEPING
12 SERVER ROOM
13 REEL STORAGE
14 ELECTRICAL
15 I.T.
16 HUMAN RESOURCES
17 FLAME BAY
18 AVID
19 CONFERENCE
20 FREELANCE DESIGNERS
21 RESEARCH LIBRARY

WONG DOODY
ADVERTISING AGENCY
CULVER CITY, CA / 2006

CHALLENGE: HOW CAN ALPINE IMPROVE
"SOUND QUALITY" IMAGE?
DEALERS.

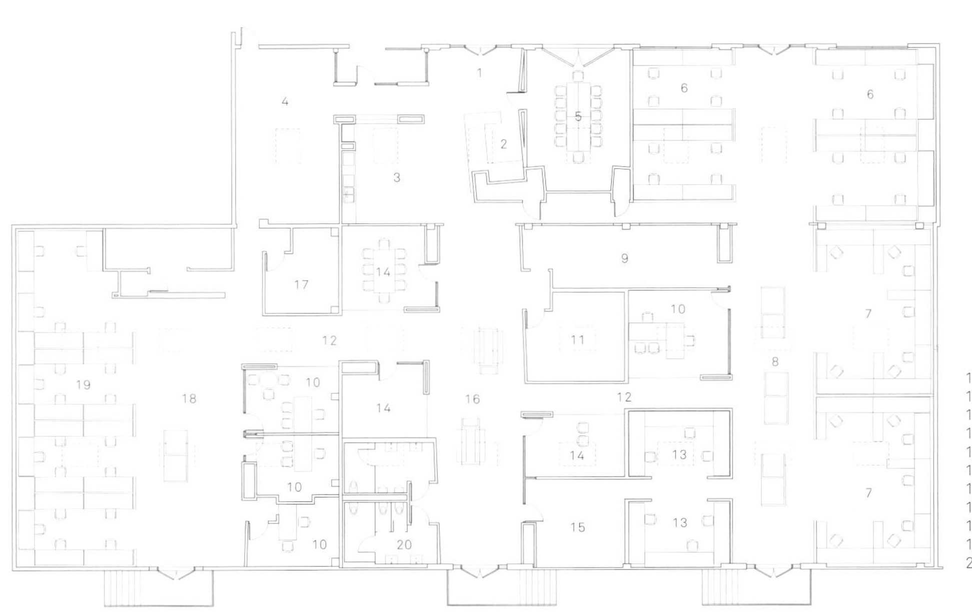
1 ENTRY
2 RECEPTION
3 BREAK ROOM
4 EMPLOYEE CHILL ZONE
5 CONFERENCE
6 ACCOUNTS BULLPEN
7 PRODUCTION BULLPEN
8 PRODUCTION LAYOUT
9 COPY/MAIL
10 OFFICE
11 MACHINE ROOM
12 GALLERY
13 CREATIVE BULLPEN
14 WAR ROOM
15 LIBRARY
16 OPEN STUDY
17 AVID
18 LAYOUT
19 INTERACTIVE BULLPEN
20 RESTROOMS

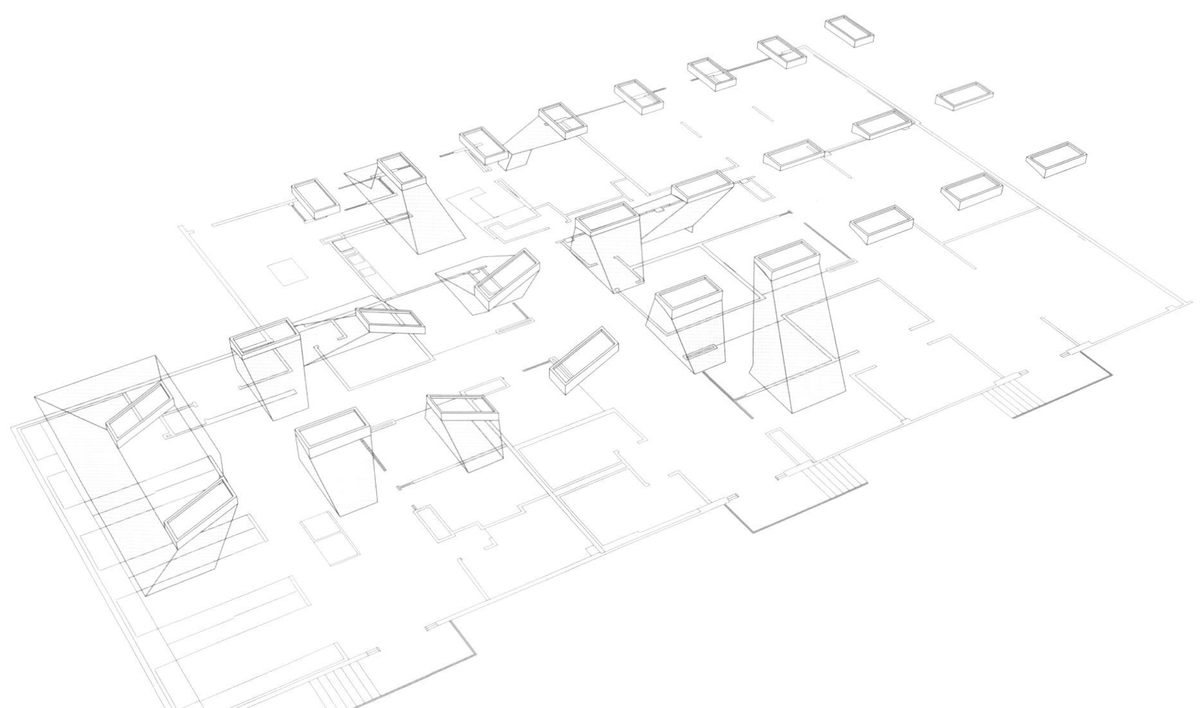

RIVIERA RESIDENCE
SANTA BARBARA, CA / 2006

SALLY MANN DEEP SOUTH
2000 YEARS OF JAPANESE ART

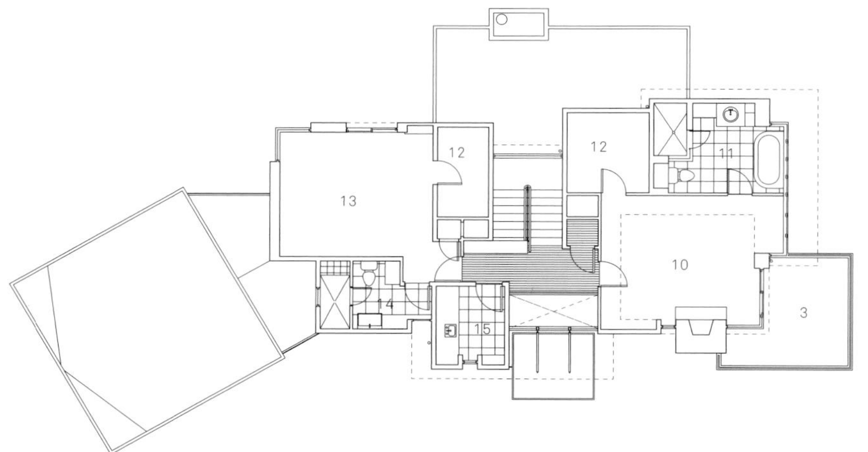

SECOND FLOOR

10 MASTER BEDROOM
11 MASTER BATH
12 CLOSET
13 BEDROOM
14 BATH
15 LAUNDRY

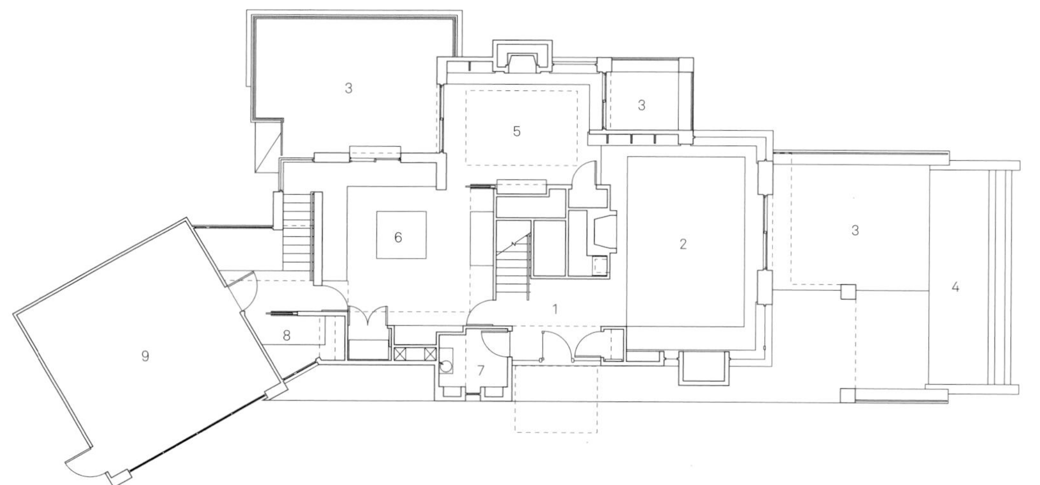

FIRST FLOOR

1 ENTRY
2 LIVING
3 DECK
4 POOL
5 DINING
6 KITCHEN
7 POWDER
8 OFFICE
9 GARAGE

NORTH
WEST

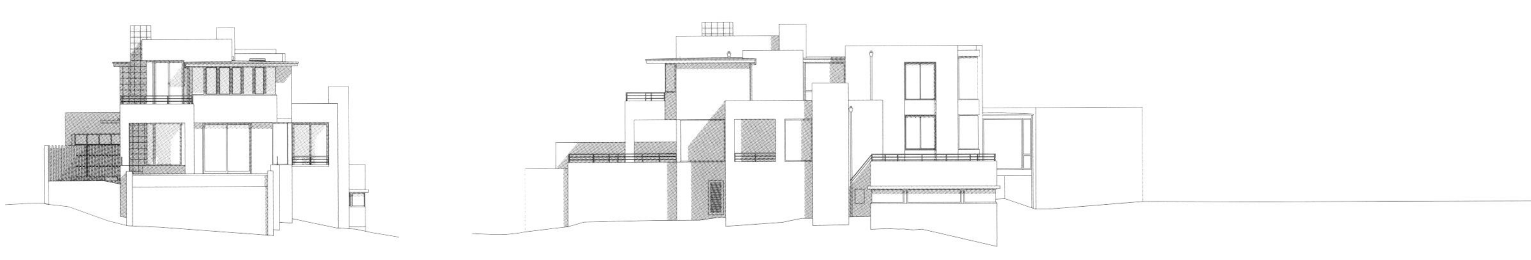

SOUTH EAST

GREENTREE RESIDENCE
PACIFIC PALISADES, CA / 2006

SECOND FLOOR

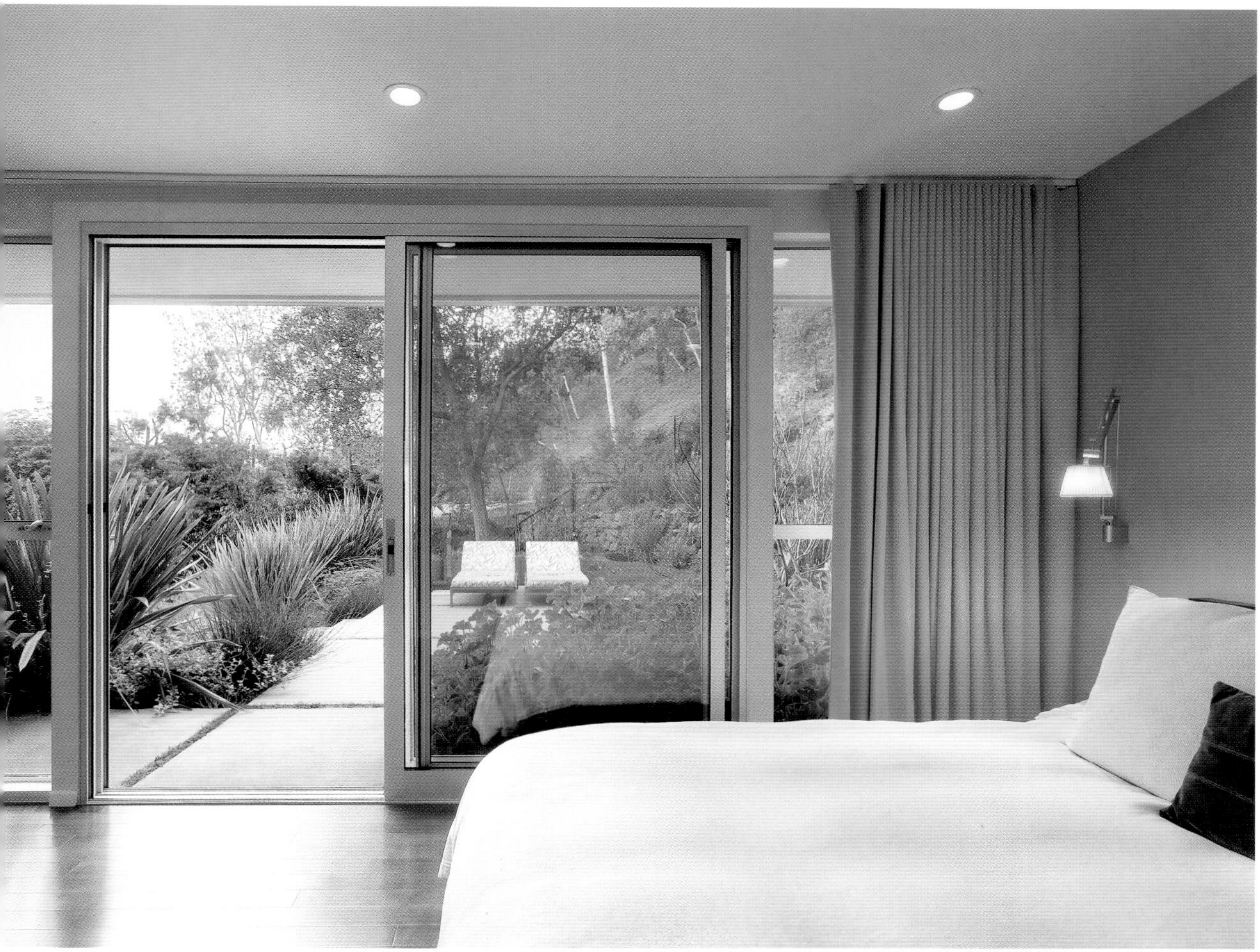

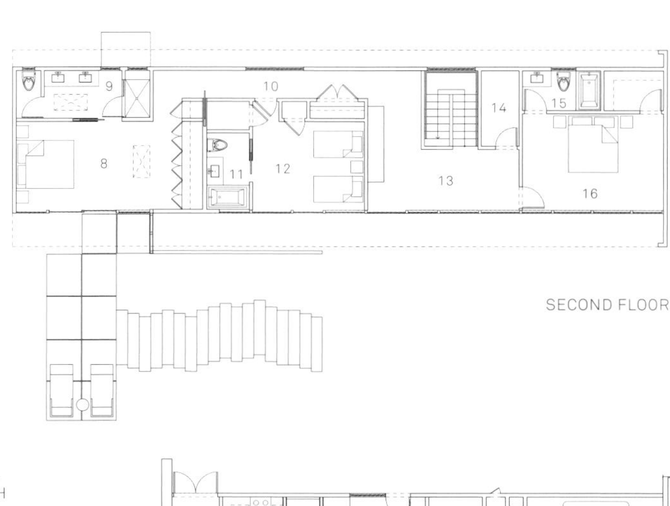

1 ENTRY
2 DINING
3 KITCHEN
4 MECHANICAL
5 POWDER BATH
6 LAUNDRY
7 LIVING
8 MASTER BEDROOM
9 MASTER BATH
10 HALL
11 BATH
12 BEDROOM
13 LOUNGE AREA
14 STORAGE
15 BATH
16 BEDROOM

FIRST FLOOR

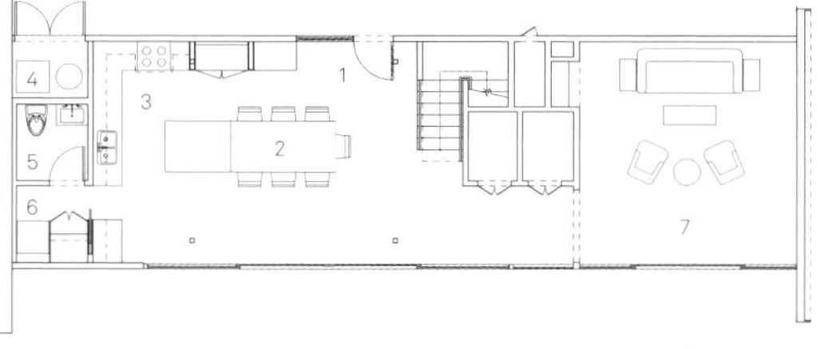

DUBAI VILLAS
DUBAI, UAE / DESIGNED 2008

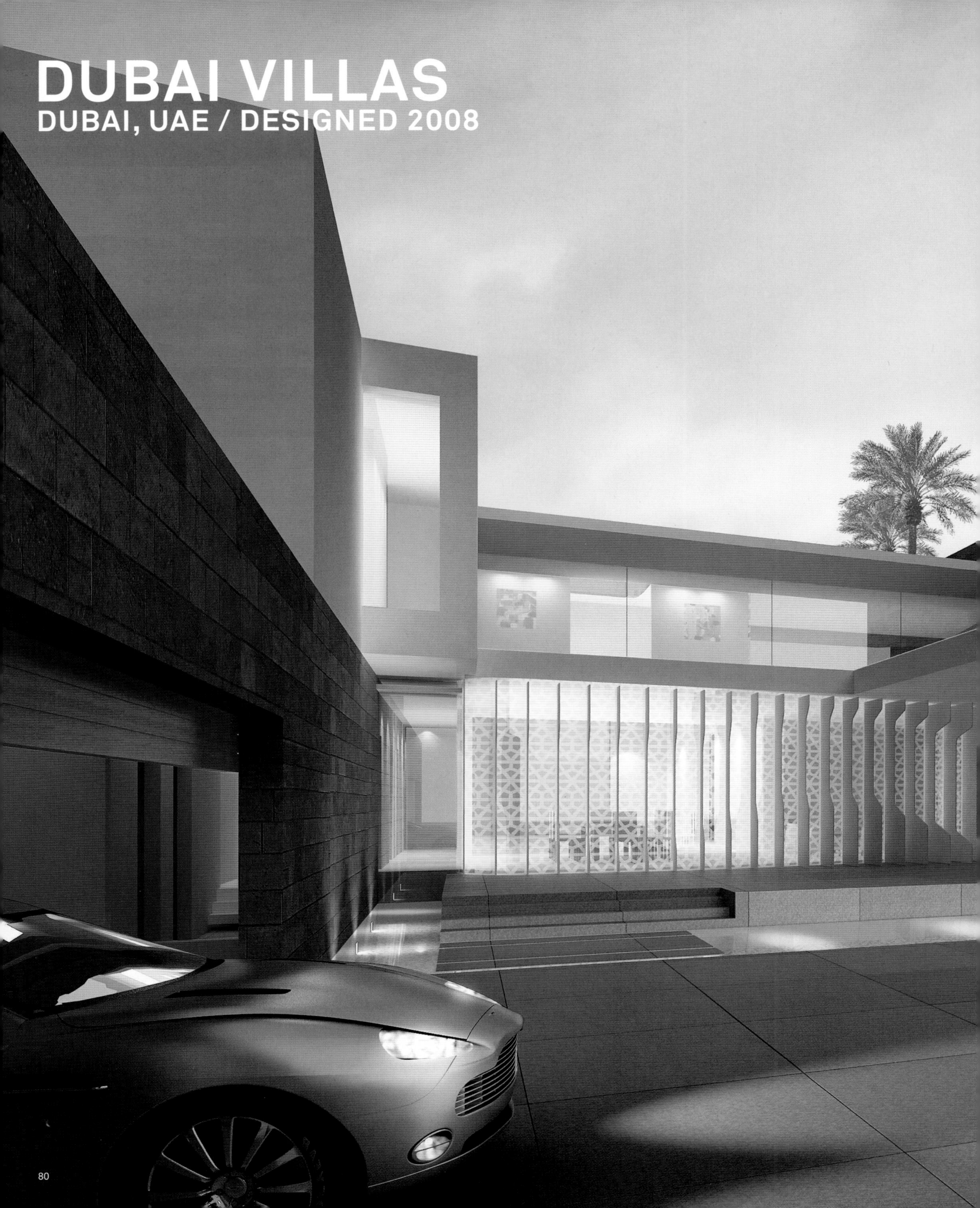

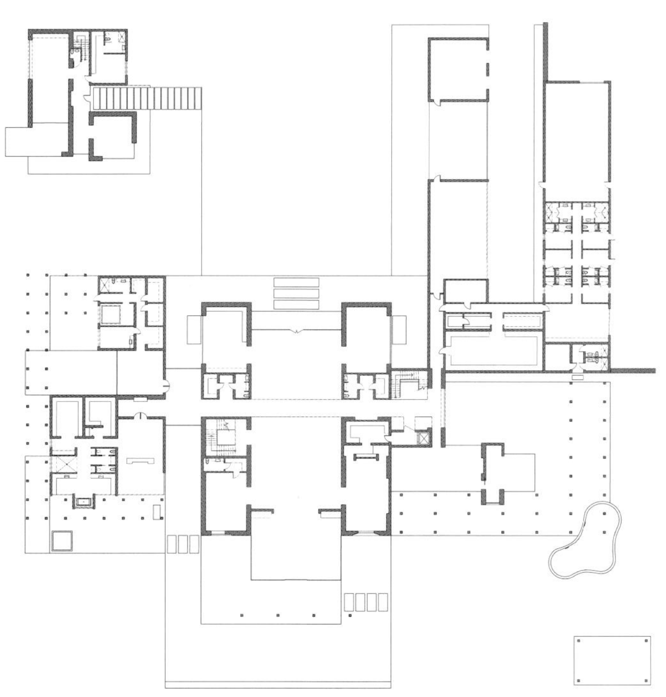

VIP VILLA

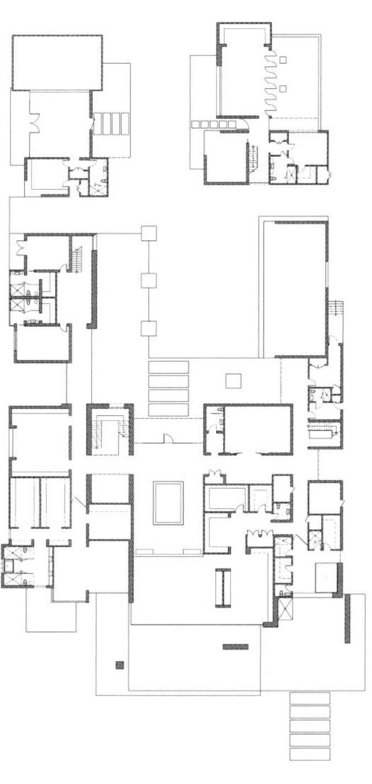

LARGE VILLA

MEDIUM VILLA

EAST CHANNEL RESIDENCE
SANTA MONICA, CA / 2009

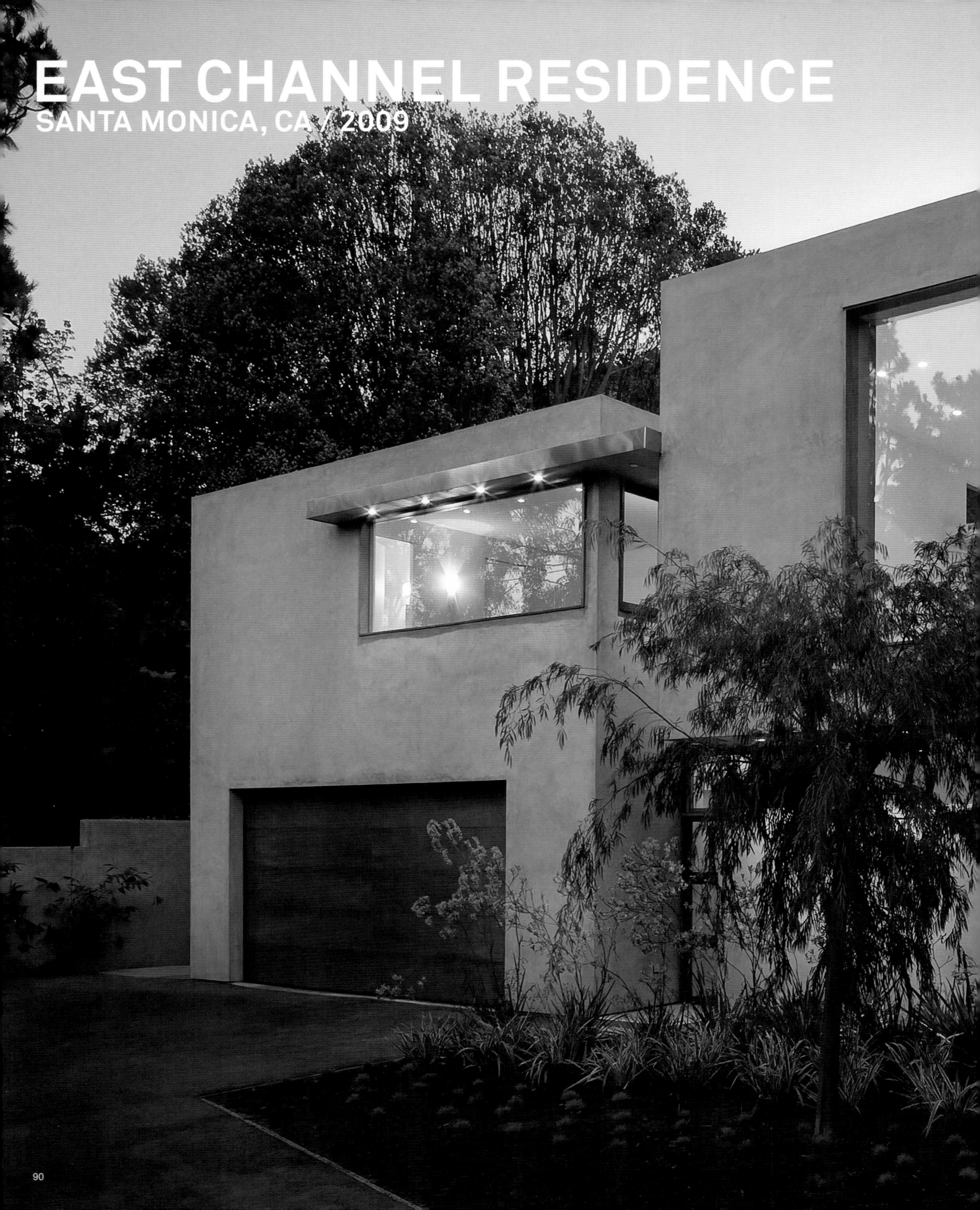

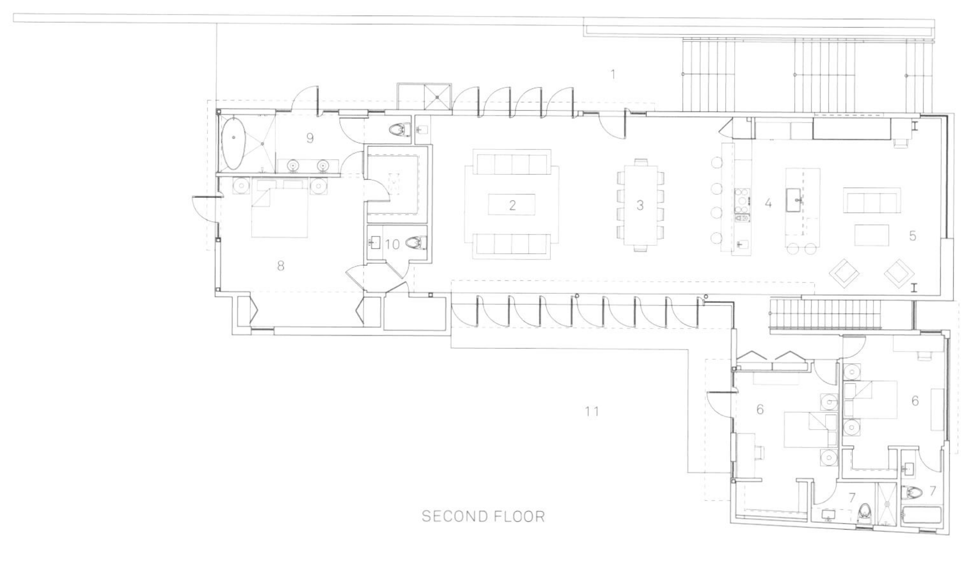

SECOND FLOOR

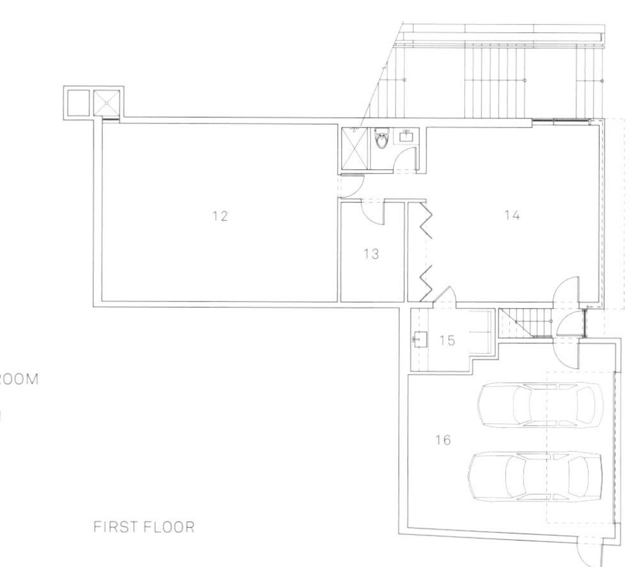

FIRST FLOOR

1 ENTRY
2 LIVING
3 DINING
4 KITCHEN
5 FAMILY
6 BEDROOM
7 BATH
8 MASTER BEDROOM
9 MASTER BATH
10 POWDER BATH
11 COURTYARD
12 STORAGE
13 WINE CELLAR
14 STUDY
15 LAUNDRY
16 GARAGE

SANTA BARBARA ESTATE

SANTA BARBARA, CA / 2003

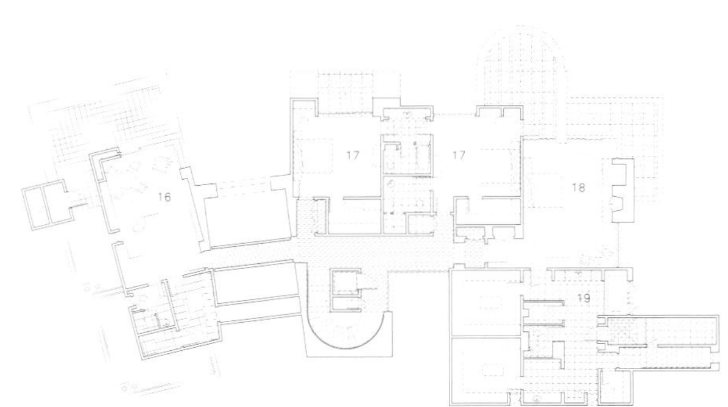

SECOND FLOOR

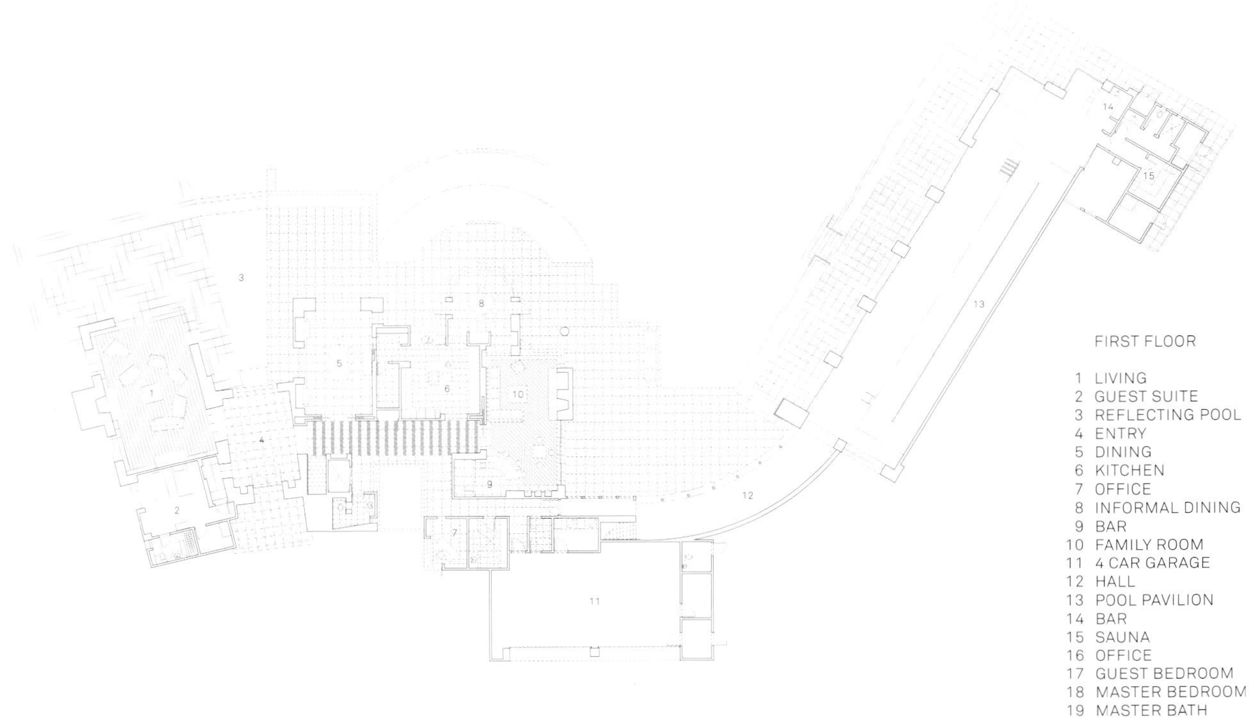

FIRST FLOOR

1 LIVING
2 GUEST SUITE
3 REFLECTING POOL
4 ENTRY
5 DINING
6 KITCHEN
7 OFFICE
8 INFORMAL DINING
9 BAR
10 FAMILY ROOM
11 4 CAR GARAGE
12 HALL
13 POOL PAVILION
14 BAR
15 SAUNA
16 OFFICE
17 GUEST BEDROOM
18 MASTER BEDROOM
19 MASTER BATH

BENTLEY RESIDENCE
BEL AIR, CA / 2007

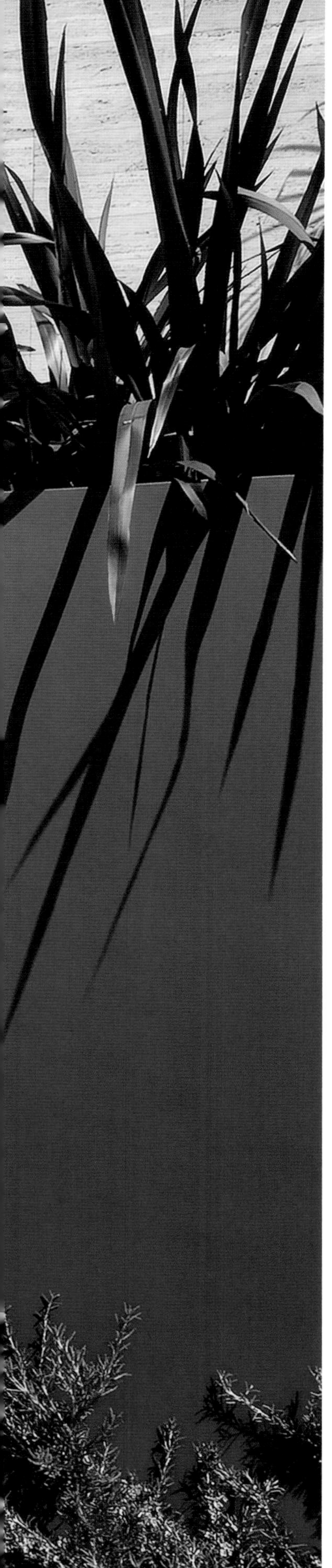

SOUTH ELEVATION

EAST ELEVATION

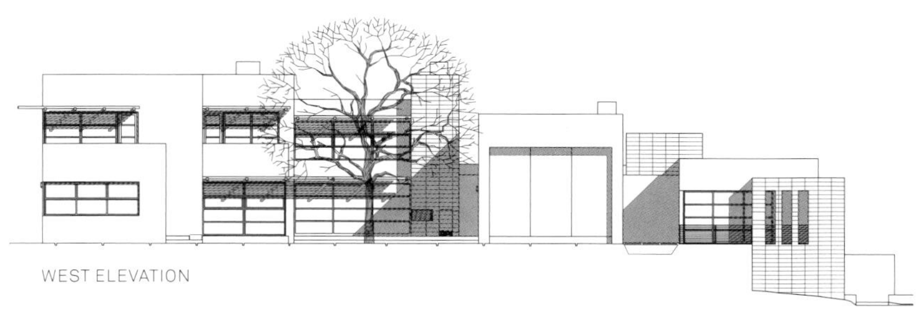

WEST ELEVATION

Andy Warhol's
Interview

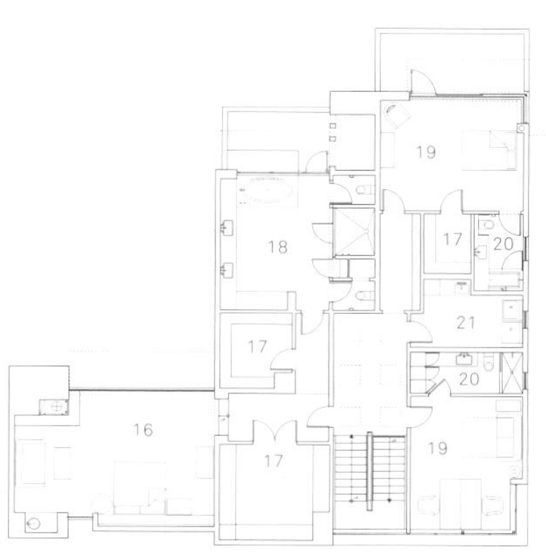

SECOND FLOOR

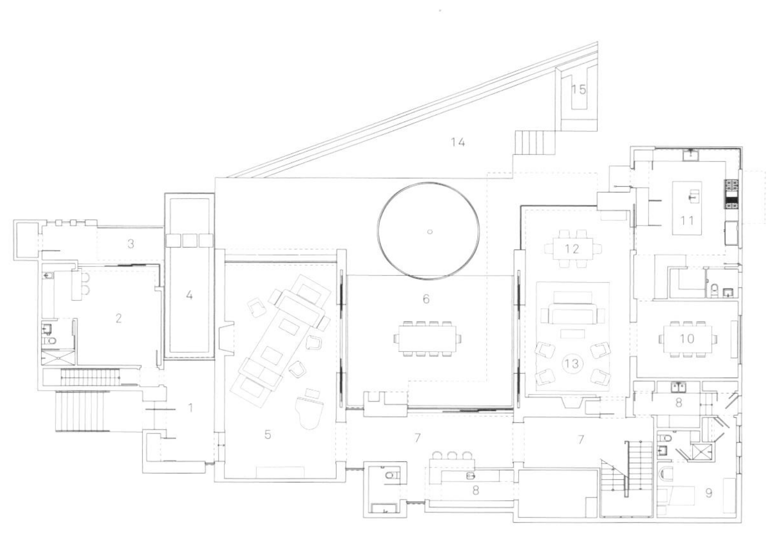

1 ENTRY
2 STUDY
3 PATIO
4 REFLECTING POOL
5 LIVING
6 COURTYARD
7 GALLERY
8 LAUNDRY
9 GUEST
10 DINING
11 KITCHEN
12 FAMILY DINING
13 FAMILY
14 POOL
15 SPA
16 MASTER BEDROOM
17 CLOSET
18 MASTER BATH
19 BEDROOM
20 BATH
21 LAUNDRY

DAVIDANDGOLIATH

ADVERTISING AGENCY
EL SEGUNDO, CA / 2006

killerspin

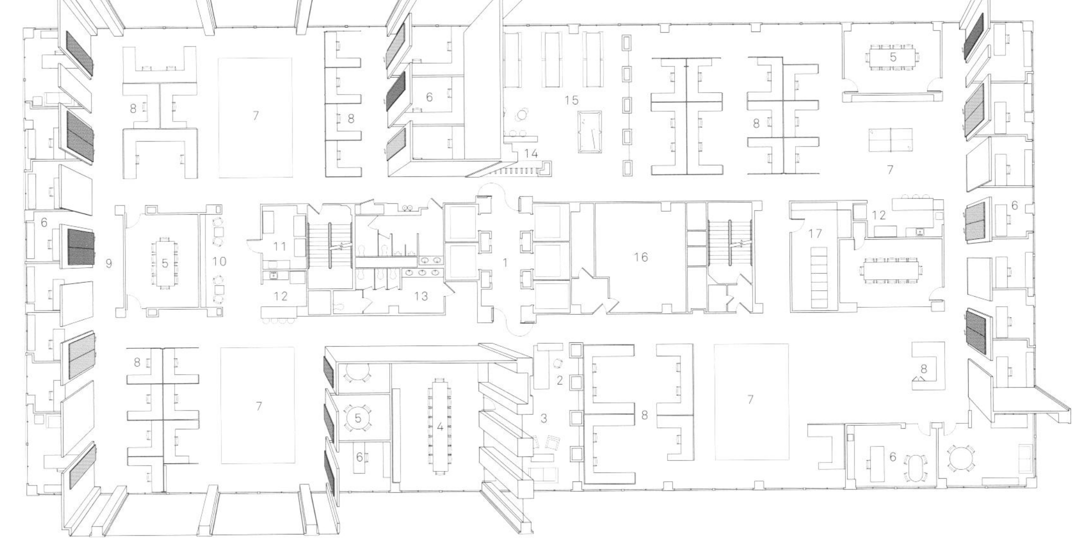

1 ELEVATOR LOBBY
2 RECEPTION
3 LOBBY
4 CONFERENCE
5 WAR ROOM
6 OFFICE
7 GATHERING AREA
8 WORK STATIONS
9 HALL / STORAGE
10 REFERENCE LIBRARY
11 COPY
12 COFFEE BAR
13 RESTROOMS
14 BAR
15 LOUNGE
16 MACHINE ROOM
17 SERVER ROOM

OGILVY & MATHER
ADVERTISING AGENCY
CULVER CITY, CA / 2000

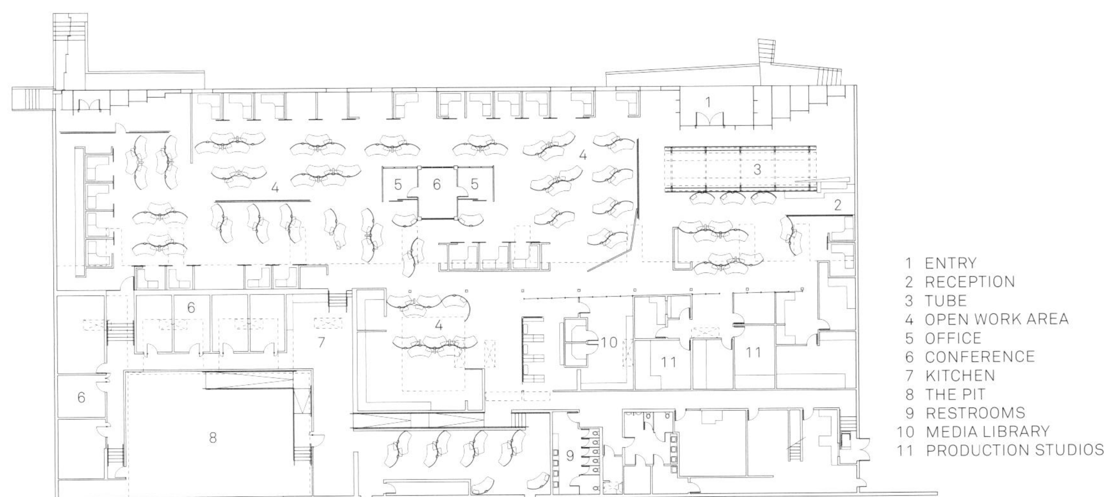
1 ENTRY
2 RECEPTION
3 TUBE
4 OPEN WORK AREA
5 OFFICE
6 CONFERENCE
7 KITCHEN
8 THE PIT
9 RESTROOMS
10 MEDIA LIBRARY
11 PRODUCTION STUDIOS

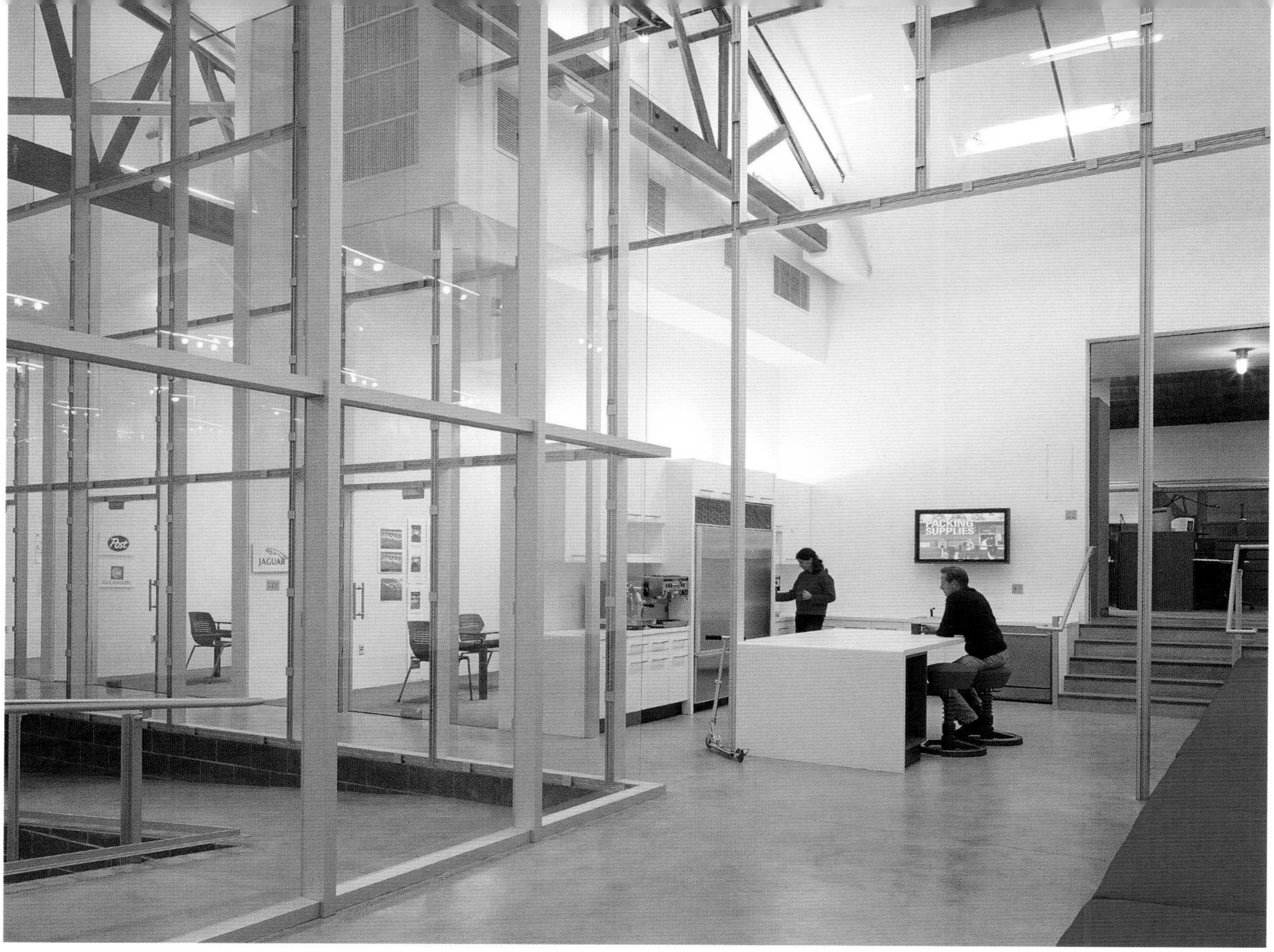
Post
JAGUAR
PACKING SUPPLIES

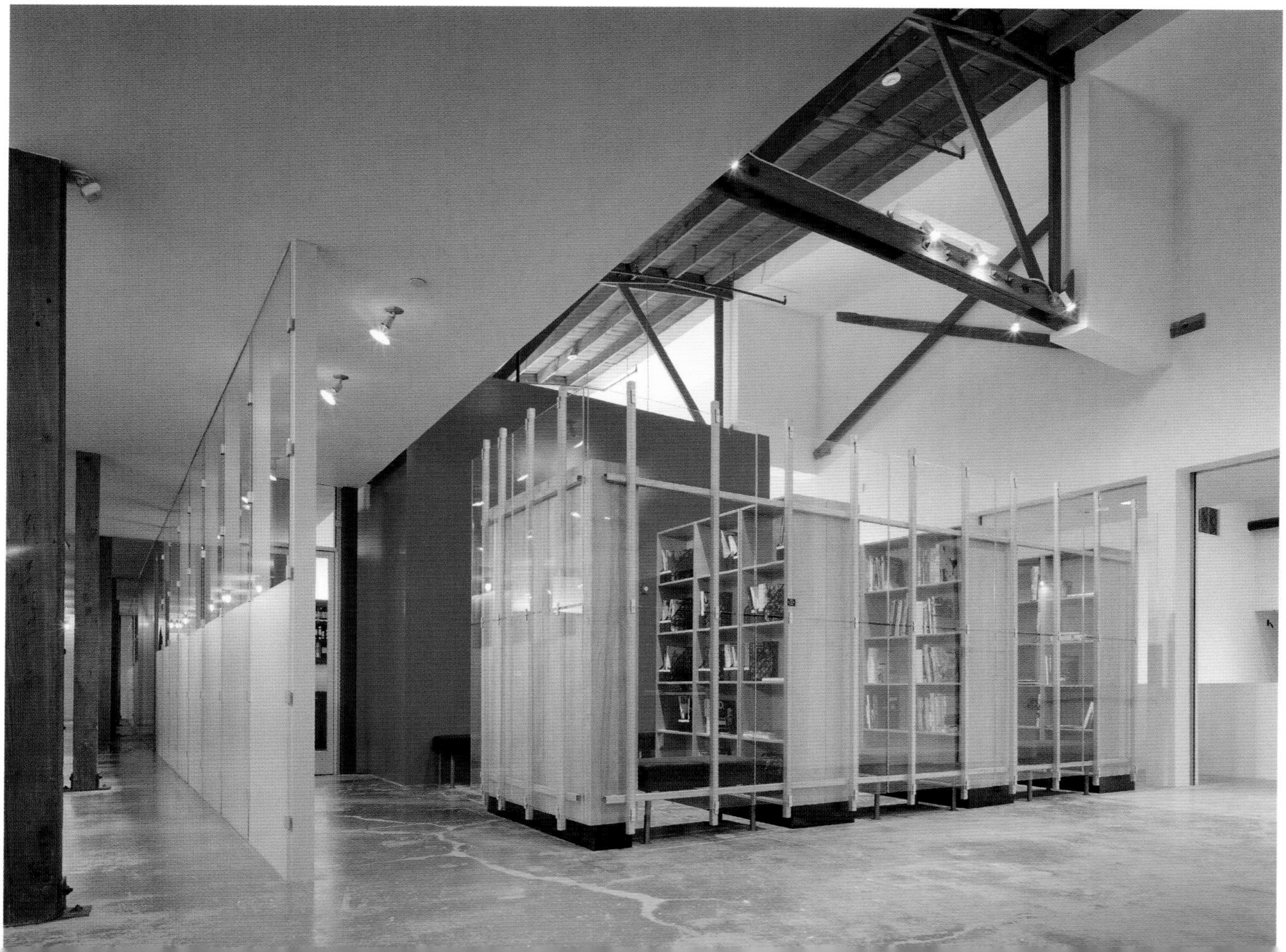

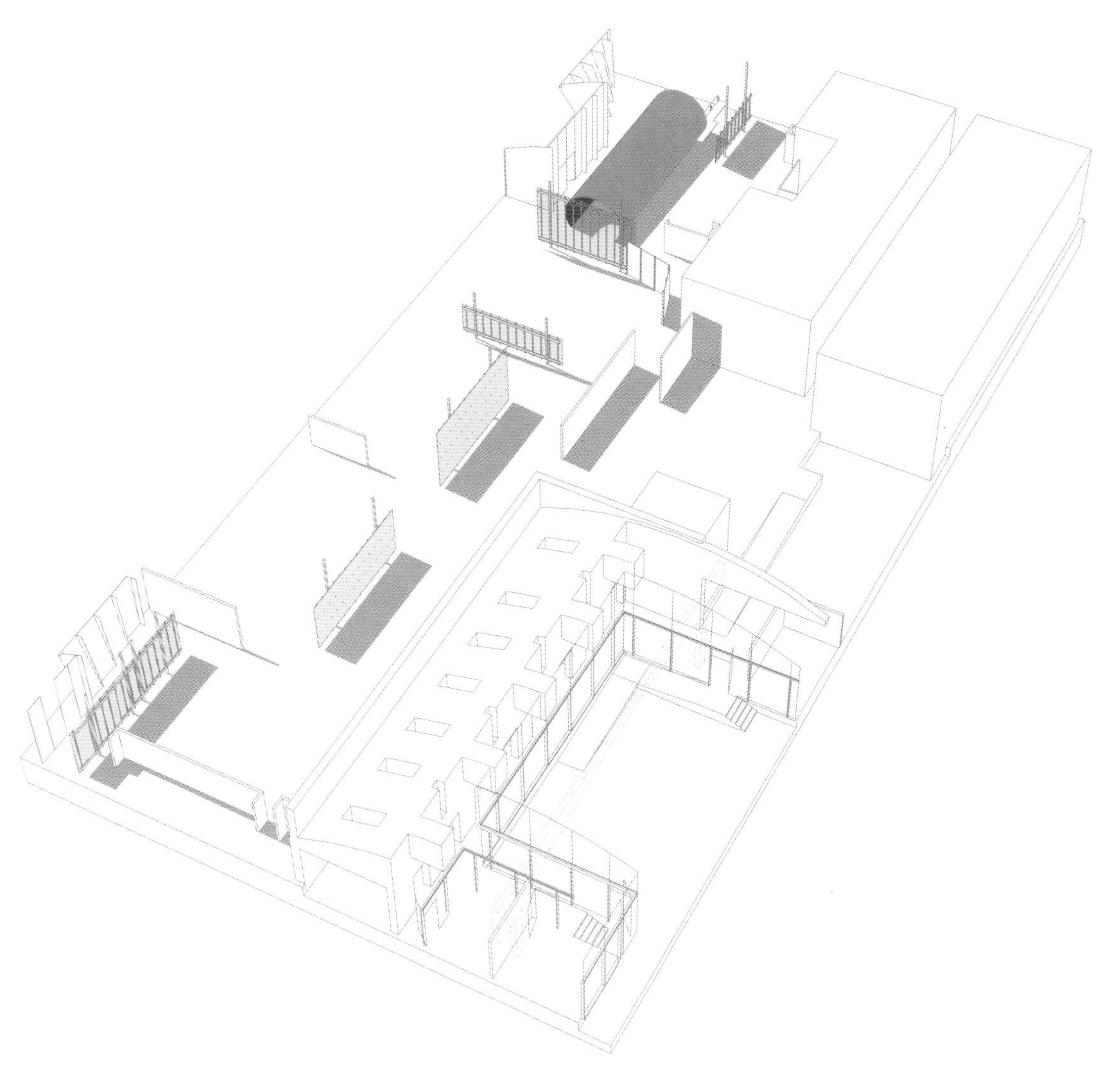

HYDRAULX

SPECIAL EFFECTS
SANTA MONICA, CA / 2007

MIDWAY

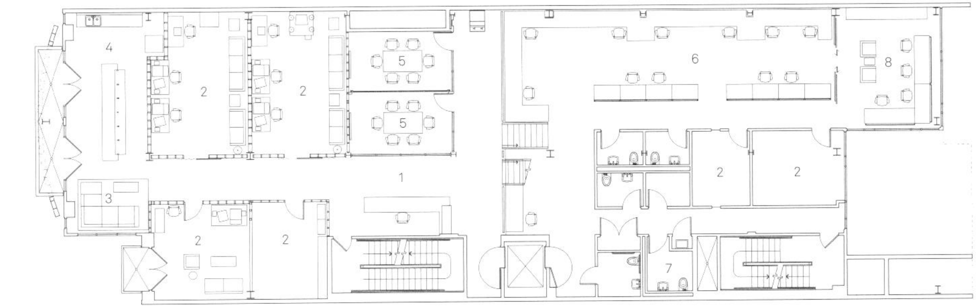

FIRST FLOOR

1 RECEPTION
2 OFFICE
3 LOUNGE
4 KITCHEN
5 WAR ROOM
6 OPEN WORK AREA
7 RESTROOMS
8 REFERENCE LIBRARY
9 SERVER ROOM

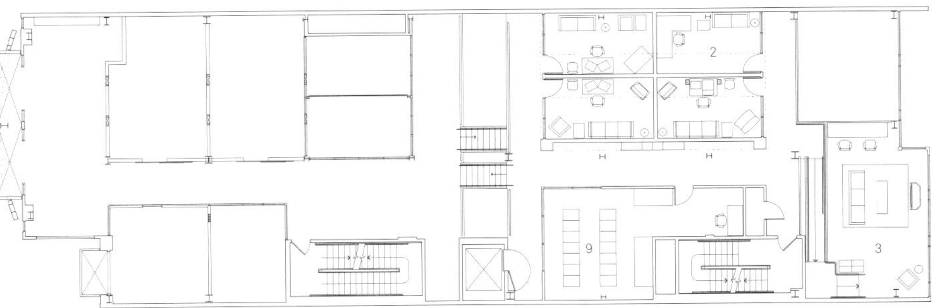

SECOND FLOOR

FUEL DESIGN & PRODUCTION

MOTION GRAPHICS
SANTA MONICA, CA / 1998

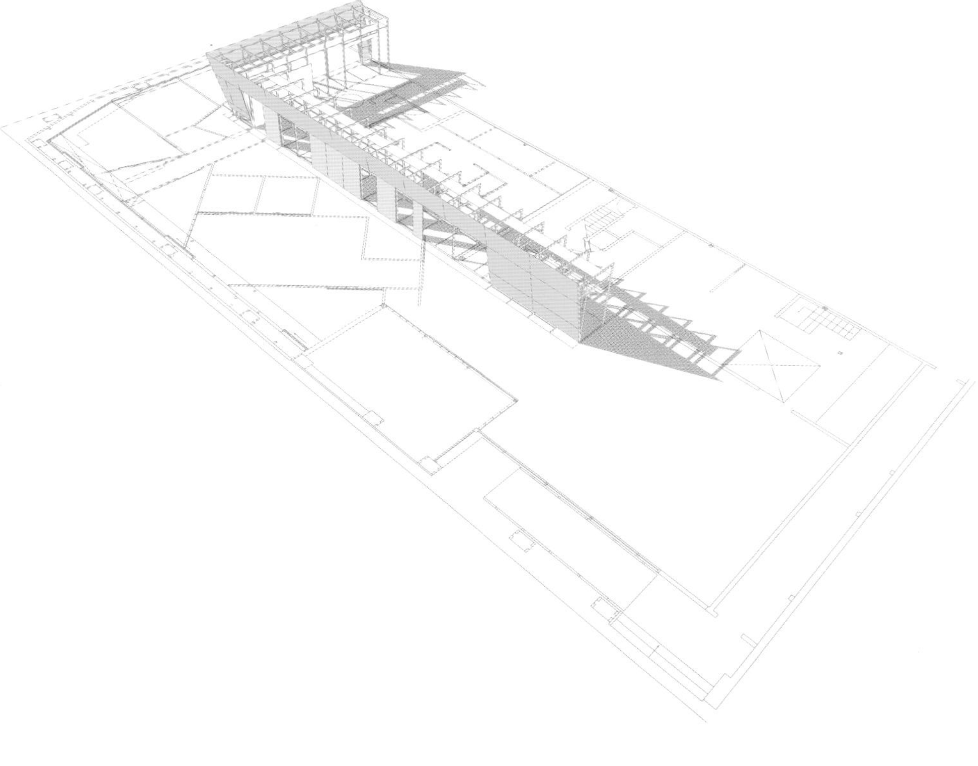

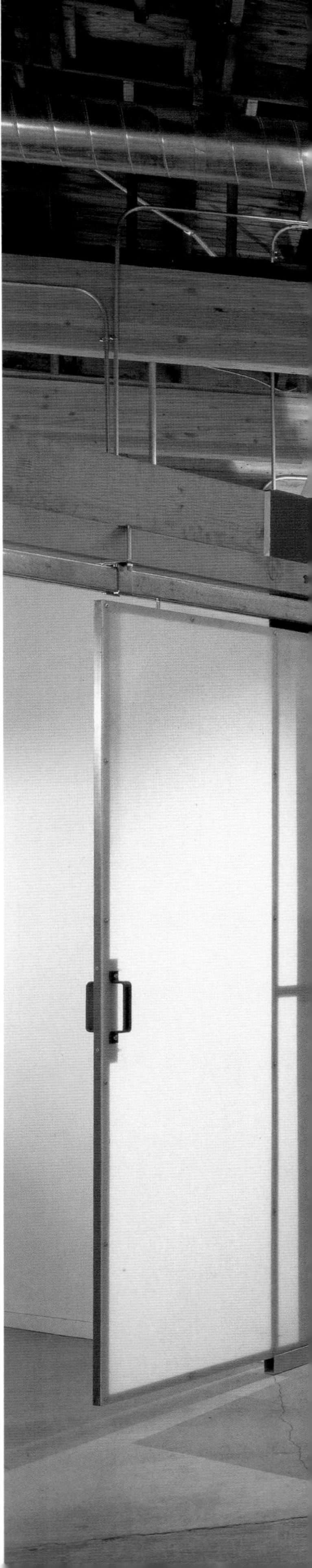

1 ENTRY
2 OFFICE
3 INFORMATION BAR
4 WORK STATIONS
5 RESTROOMS
6 CONFERENCE
7 KITCHEN
8 LOUNGE

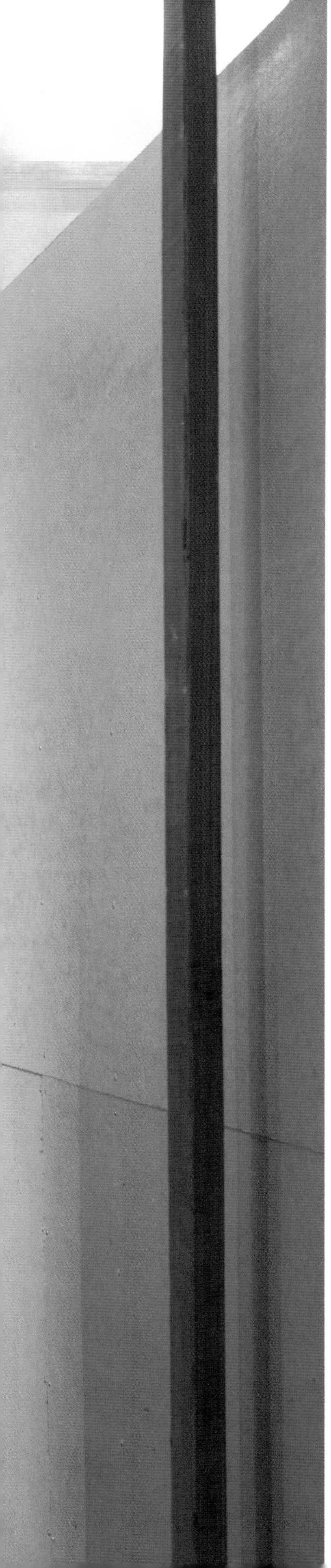

ARTIST STUDIO
SANTA BARBARA, CA / 2002

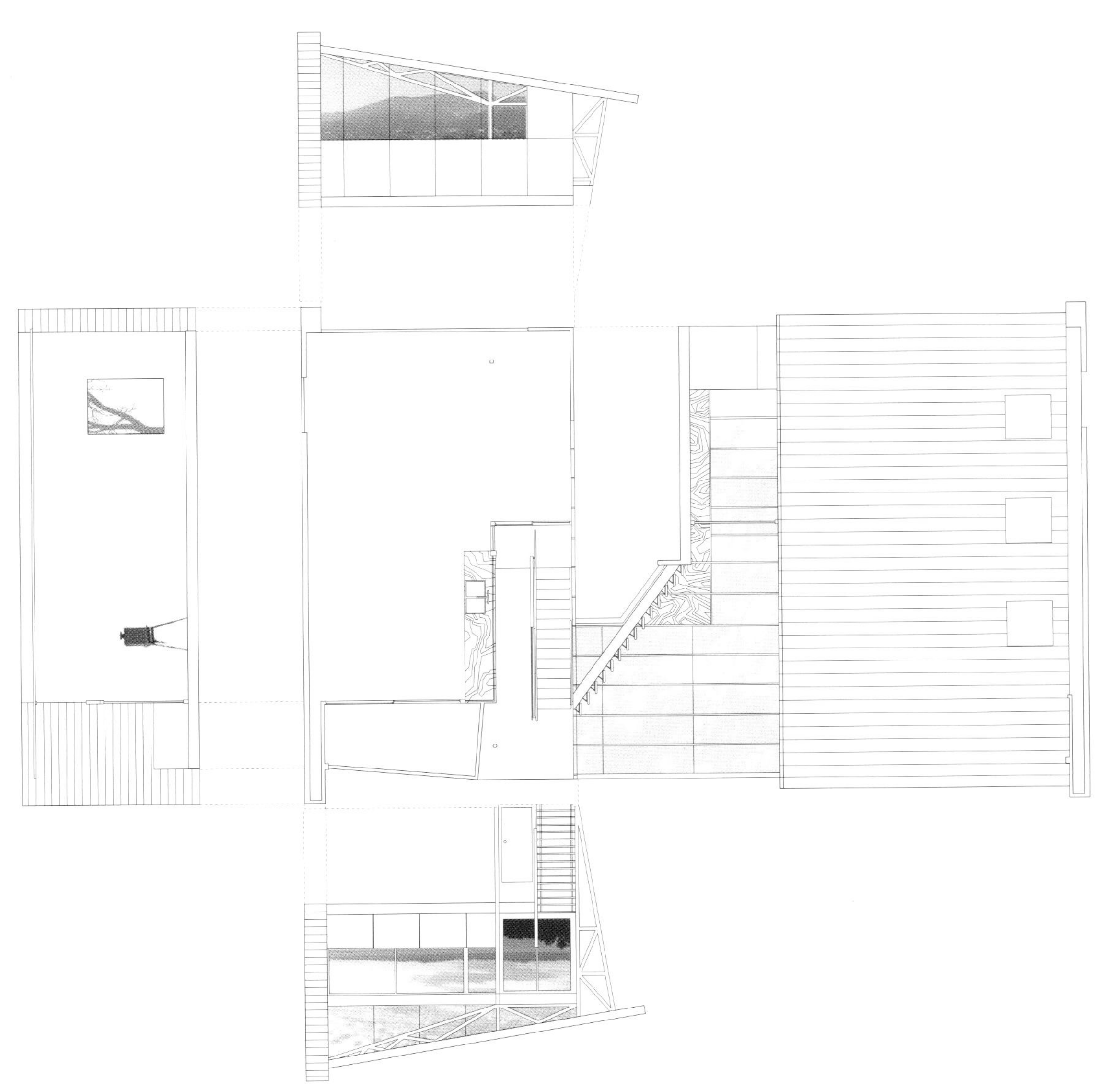

SAATCHI & SAATCHI

ADVERTISING AGENCY
TORRANCE, CA / 2008

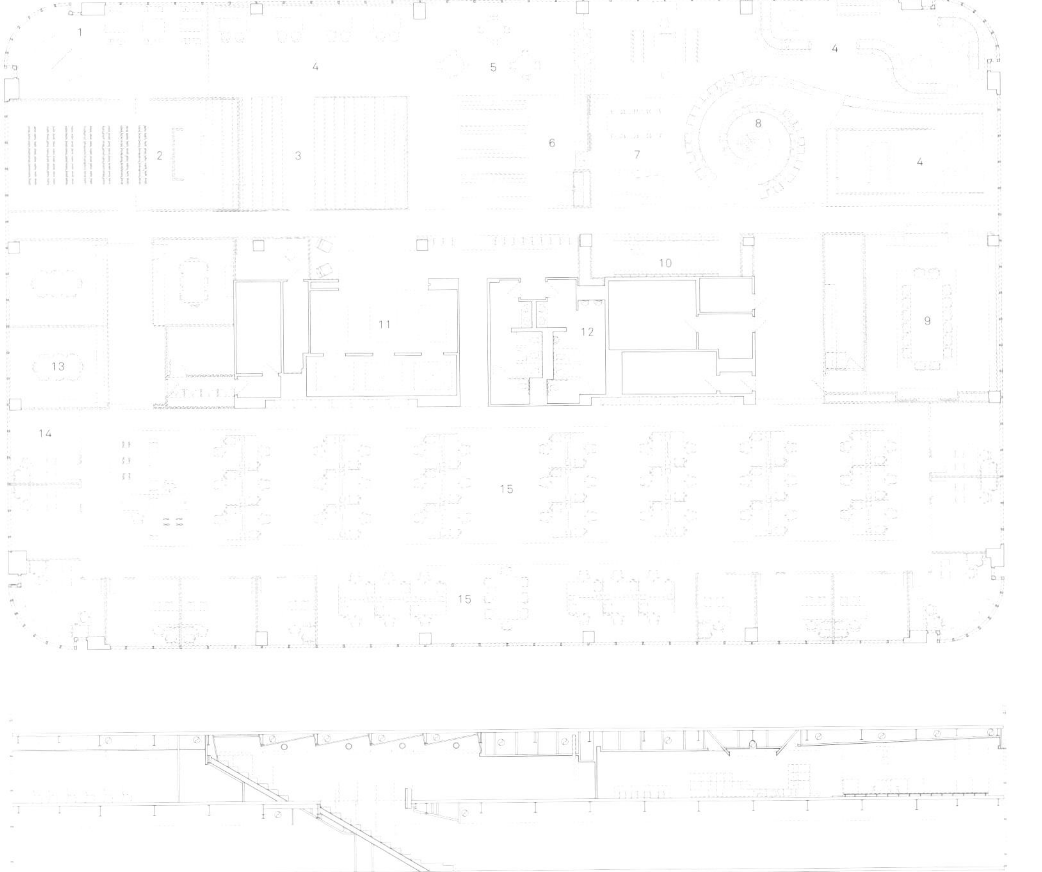

THIRD FLOOR

1 "REC ROOM"
2 SISOMO ROOM
3 GRAND STAIR MEETING AREA
4 FOCUS AREA
5 "DINING ROOM"
6 BREAK ROOM / KITCHEN
7 "GAME ROOM"
8 LIBRARY
9 CONFERENCE
10 BAR
11 ELEVATOR / LOBBY
12 RESTROOMS
13 WAR ROOM
14 OFFICE
15 WORK AREA

BISCUIT FILMWORKS
FILM PRODUCTION
HOLLYWOOD, CA / 2009

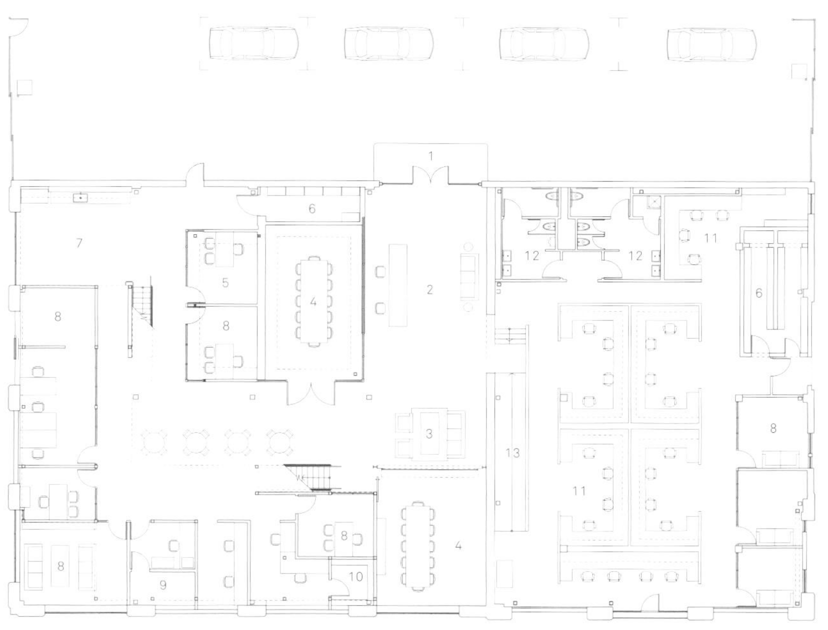

1 ENTRY
2 RECEPTION
3 LOUNGE
4 CONFERENCE
5 LIBRARY
6 STORAGE
7 KITCHEN
8 OFFICE
9 SERVER
10 VAULT
11 PRODUCTION BAY
12 RESTROOM
13 RAMP

27
ANDO

TORO CANYON RESIDENCE
SANTA BARBARA, CA / 2009

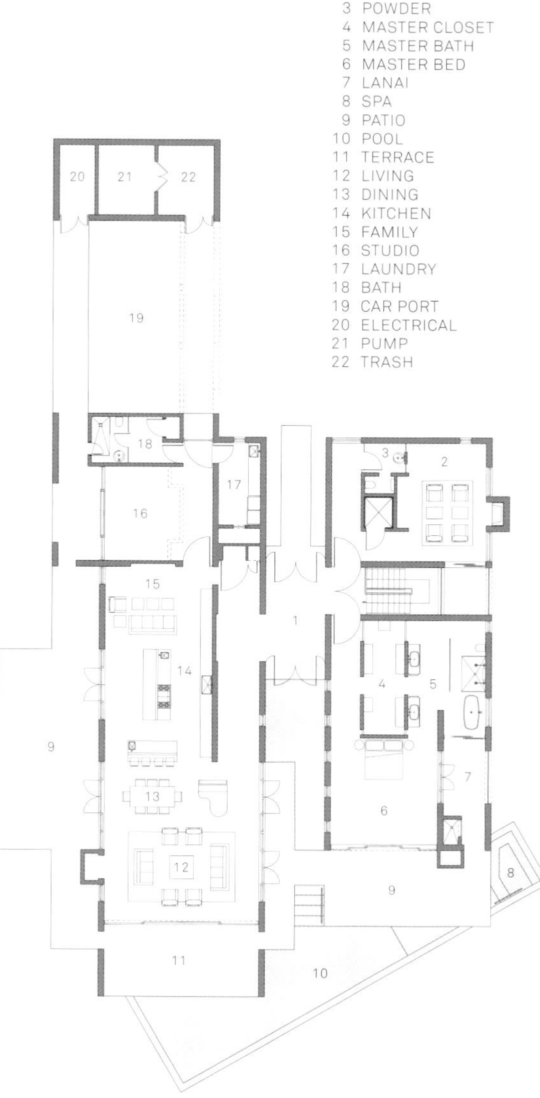
1 ENTRY
2 OFFICE
3 POWDER
4 MASTER CLOSET
5 MASTER BATH
6 MASTER BED
7 LANAI
8 SPA
9 PATIO
10 POOL
11 TERRACE
12 LIVING
13 DINING
14 KITCHEN
15 FAMILY
16 STUDIO
17 LAUNDRY
18 BATH
19 CAR PORT
20 ELECTRICAL
21 PUMP
22 TRASH

THE FIRM
TALENT AGENCY
BEVERLY HILLS, CA / 2002

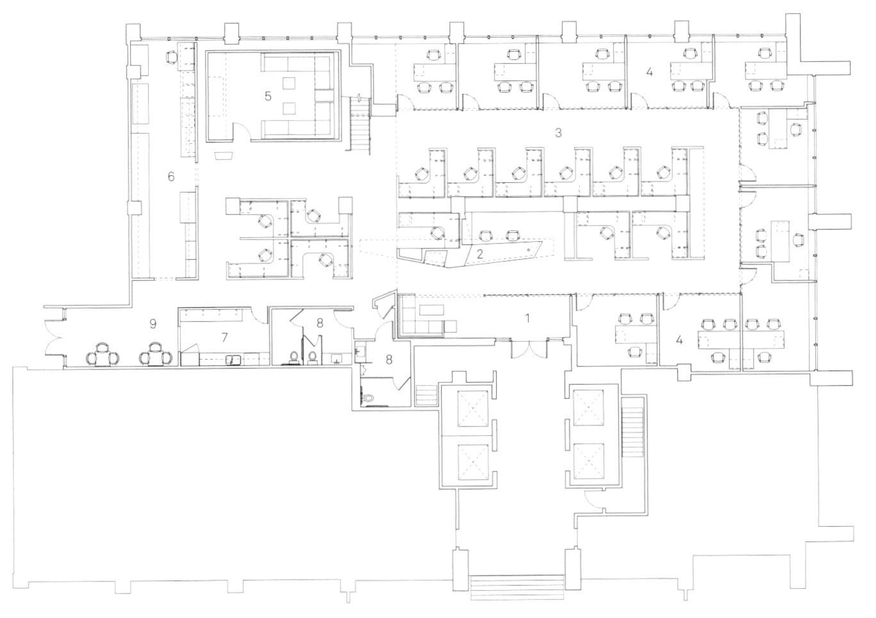

1 ENTRY
2 RECEPTION
3 OPEN WORK AREA
4 OFFICE
5 CONFERENCE
6 STORAGE
7 KITCHEN
8 RESTROOMS
9 LOUNGE

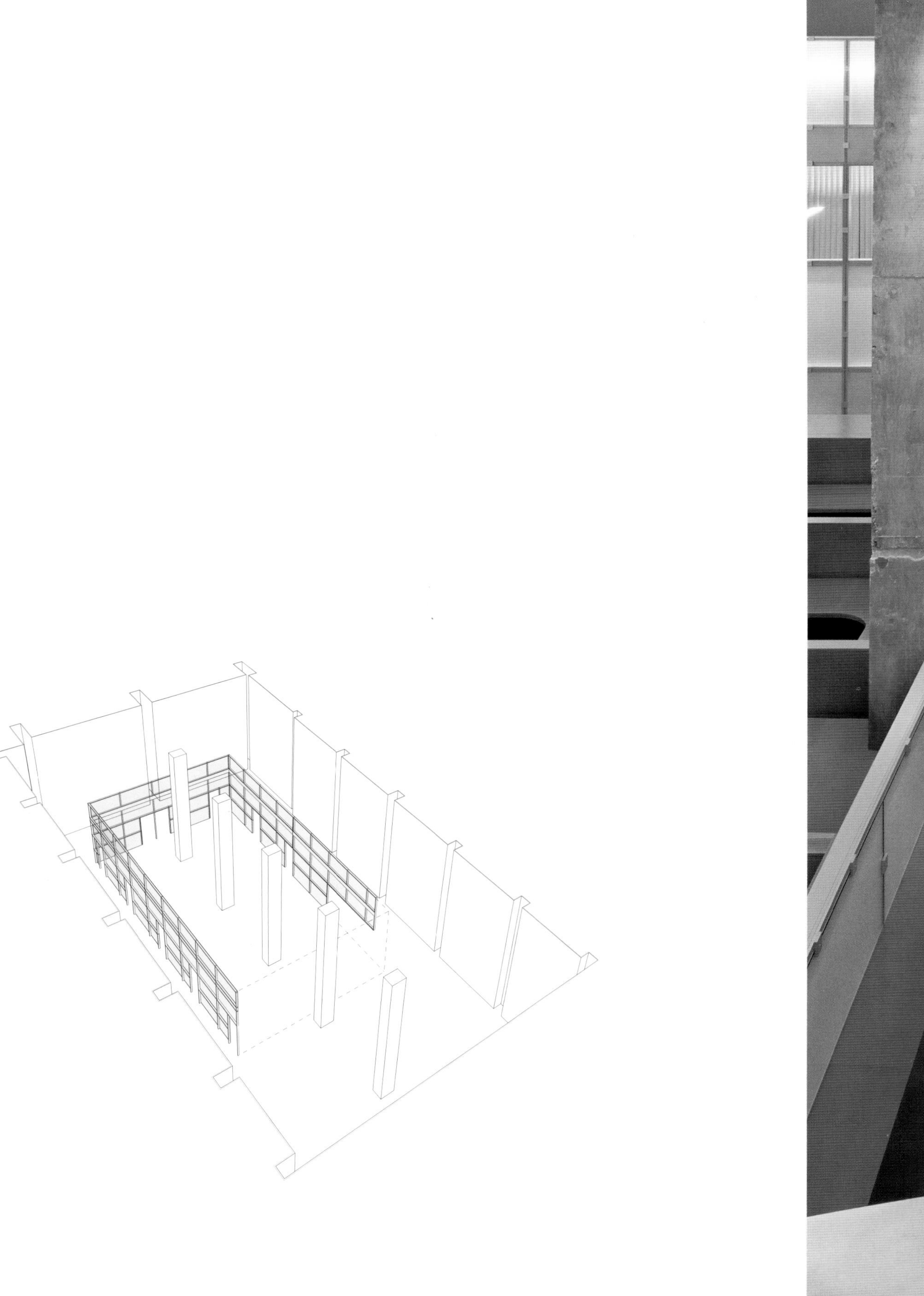

PAINTER RESIDENCE
BEL AIR, CA / DESIGNED 2006

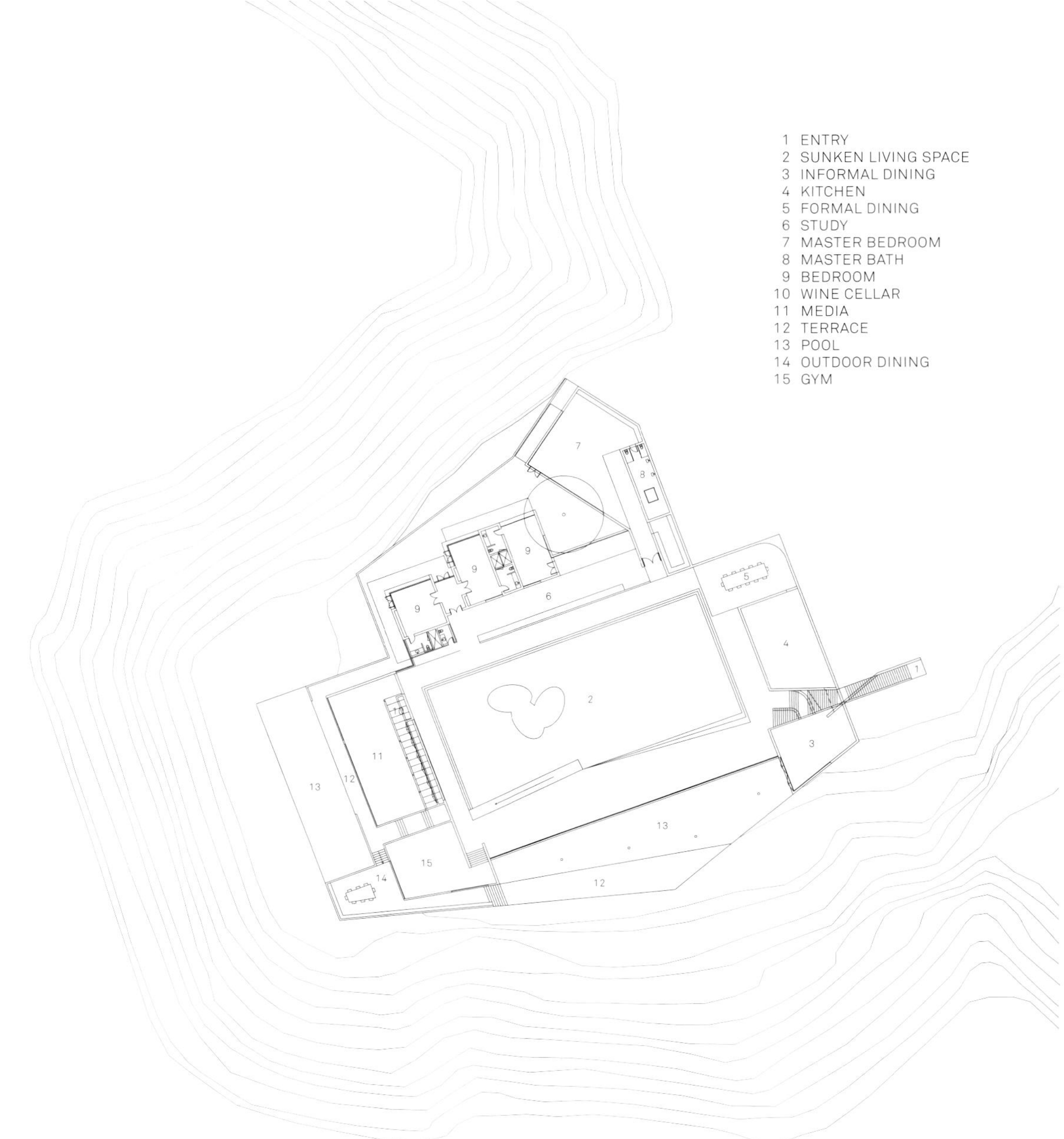
1 ENTRY
2 SUNKEN LIVING SPACE
3 INFORMAL DINING
4 KITCHEN
5 FORMAL DINING
6 STUDY
7 MASTER BEDROOM
8 MASTER BATH
9 BEDROOM
10 WINE CELLAR
11 MEDIA
12 TERRACE
13 POOL
14 OUTDOOR DINING
15 GYM

A CHOREOGRAPHY OF COLLISION
THOM MAYNE

At home with the ephemeral – the found, the ad hoc, the messiness of reality Shubin + Donaldson's work transmits a distinct immediacy – an expressive energy that emerges from the spontaneity of the creative process. The architecture maintains a direct engagement with the raw reality of creative production; nothing has been overworked. The spontaneous architecture connects with thought processes that take place in the media agencies it houses – associative and loose. Open-ended and malleable, the spaces cultivate creativity through happenstance and chance collisions.

At these moments of collision, rich juxtapositions between found elements and contemporary innovations emerge, linking the work of Shubin + Donaldson to Robert Rauschenberg's Combines or Merce Cunningham's choreography of chance operations. For Rauschenberg, rather than the purity contained in abstract painting, it was the impurity of hybrid art – the collectiveness and surprise of found objects not separate from daily life – that produced new and infinite possibilities for experiencing our contemporary environment. At the moment of collision – when delineated boundaries between art and sculpture, as well as art and life, were broken down and combined into a single work of art – a sense of discovery, excitement, and adventure emerged. It is this inventiveness of the Combines, the open-ended and unfinished quality, the dependence on chance, possibility and uncertainty that embodies the richness of Shubin + Donaldson's work.

Shubin + Donaldson establish relationships among a diverse collection of materials by layering, association, and juxtaposition, rather than through composition or geometry. Beyond physical materials and found industrial artifacts, intangible elements, such as light, 2-D graphics, digital imagery, and film, act quite literally as building materials. Distinctions between primary, secondary, and tertiary elements blur, as a concrete ramp becomes a desk, as fragments of walls are overlaid with graphic imagery, and light translucent materials intersect massive industrial elements.

Shubin + Donaldson choreographs experiences, materials, and collisions to narrate a cinematic experience through space. Like the early work of Rauschenberg and the artist's collaborations with Cunningham, the process of composing based on chance procedures – exploring relationships in the same time and space, but creating productions of art, dance, music, and architecture in isolation of one another – evokes an experience that is immediate and visceral. One must move through the spaces of Shubin + Donaldson to grasp them. The layered, tactile architecture elicits a 'creative awakening' of the senses, to borrow graphic designer Kenya Hara's definition of haptic design. Direct sense perception takes precedence over intellectual understanding.

SENSE AND SENSIBILITY
JOSEPH GIOVANNINI

The apparent placelessness of Los Angeles, where one community bleeds into another with little visible distinction, can partially be attributed to its major industries – advertising, television, movies, the web – because these businesses live placelessly, mostly in periodicals, or on screens in the theater, in the family room, and at the desk. Their buildings have no need to manifest public presence or exhibit civic responsibility via architecture: the mission of the structures is not to shape or mark public space because the cultures they support are dispersive. Unlike a newspaper building, their headquarters are not charged with a responsibility to a constituency that lives within driving distance. Los Angeles' local industries instead are national and global, and few studios and networks have looked to architects to create a sense of place with structures that build the civic and urban character of the place. They do not put a 'there' there.

Only recently have entrepreneurs of Los Angeles' entertainment and advertising industries understood that there is a physical site appropriate for talent as well as the virtual site on the screen and in periodicals. Entertainment and its corollary industries are endemic to Southern California, and over the past decade entrepreneurs of LA's creativity factories have started to commission architects to create physical settings appropriate for their function as think tanks, talent banks, and Petri dishes to encourage and incite their occupants. Many of these entrepreneurs have abandoned the conventional pin-striped corporate offices along Wilshire, in Century City, and Downtown, in favor of adaptively re-using cavernous, bow-trussed warehouses in which the mind seems to expand to the space allowed. Found buildings have been transformed from working structures into spirited antechambers of creativity. Talent is as talent does.

Conventional architectural programs usually specify functional requirements, but these commissions require a certain quality of spirit, or what hipper talents call "juice." These are high-energy, high-IQ environments that encourage their occupants to be and think differently. Businesses that sell creativity like a commodity on the futures market have realized that architectural creativity in the workplace is both a self-advertisement and a self-fulfilling environment, and they have sought architectural firms that can use the new license and fulfill their expectations.

Established in 1991 by Russell Shubin and Robin Donaldson, Shubin + Donaldson Architects came in on the ground floor of designing these creative spaces with a series of interiors built from the mid-1990s. Even as they raised the bar for this new building type, the commissions set the pace within the office, establishing a creative agenda affecting all the other work. Residential commissions in Los Angeles have traditionally represented the arena in which Southern California architects test new ideas, but these creative venues proved for the Culver City and Santa Barbara firm a catalyst for innovation that superseded residential commissions as the cauldrons of their architectural creativity. People who might otherwise feel comfy in a Tudor home were open to the prospect of brainstorming in a creative work space, where the environmental climate might incite them to pick up a basketball and throw it at a hoop hanging in the corridor. The work place was liberative.

Shubin + Donaldson was well prepared to wield the creative license, especially since Donaldson, who was graduated from grad school at SCI-Arc in its perfervid years and worked in the offices of Morphosis, had closely studied the work of Los Angeles Light and Space artists, arguably the prime spiritual mentors of California's art scene. He cites the influence of light artists Robert Irwin, Larry Bell, James Turrell, and the New Yorkers, Richard Serra, and Dan Flavin. In the spirit of the times, when the purity of self-contained disciplines was being challenged, the architects were already predisposed to folding another field into architecture, cross-pollinating architecture with other ways of thinking. Donaldson was especially interested in the music of Brian Eno, who laid sound tracks over each other to compose dense, complex, layered music; while Shubin drew from sources with more physical manifestations/embodiment. The 1986 Jonathan Borofsky show, All is One, at the recently opened Geffen Contemporary at MoCA in downtown Los Angeles was a particularly galvanizing encounter; where Shubin identified with the immediacy of an immersive experience, the

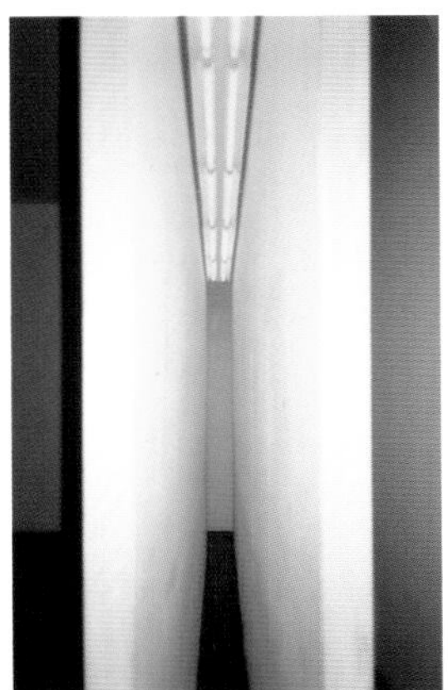

TOP BRUCE NAUMAN. GREEN LIGHT CORRIDOR. 1970. INSTALLATION AT THE VILLA PANZA. VARESE, ITALY. PHOTO COURTESY ROBIN DONALDSON. **BOTTOM** JONATHAN BOROFSKY. ALL IS ONE. 1986. INSTALLATION AT THE GEFFEN MUSEUM OF CONTEMPORARY ART, LOS ANGELES. PHOTO COURTESY JONATHAN BOROFSKY & PAULA COOPER GALLERY, NY.

exaggerated tactility of full-scale construction, and a clarity of material expression. Shubin's sensibilities have largely been directed toward how an idea comes about in the moment of doing; by working directly on the object. This process, which in some ways, is closer to that of a sculptor, is clear in many of the early commercial projects where aggressive deadlines and tight budgets forced the partners to work directly on the existing buildings, testing materials and construction methods on site, in an improvisational manner.

For Shubin + Donaldson the commission that proved the springboard into this creative world, and a break-out project within the firm's portfolio, was the low-budget commission to fast-track headquarters of Fuel Design and Production, a producer of television commercials and video graphics, in an 8,000-sq.ft. warehouse in Santa Monica, two blocks from the beach. The architects had six weeks and $30/sq. ft. to deliver the key to their clients.

Certain parameters drove the commission. The basic space was a voluminous, bow-truss structure that already provided the first requirement of a building – shelter – liberating the design inside from any obligations to shield occupants from the weather. The second "driver" was attitude: the very hands-on client wanted visitors to understand the spontaneous, flexible, can-do, unexpected, resourceful, off-center, unvarnished culture of the company just by walking through the door. The architects had to build a space that embodied the attitude and supported the business. Hand-me-down design formulas would not suffice, and precedent could not substitute for originality, even if the precedent looked like a Frank Gehry. The budget and time frame would not allow the design to be fussy or the materials, rich.

Fuel itself was specialized in edgy computer animation, motion graphics and digital design. The company's aesthetic, the deliberate result of digital layering, suggested an architectural look and process, and the architects, who were already working on the computer, decided to explore and exploit the screen for answers to the architectural question of how best to build to suit this company. The architects wanted to incorporate in the architecture the character of the company's digitally generated work, which in turn suggested the use of the computer in ways unanticipated by standard architectural software.

Instead of modeling form on a Mac with 3-D architecture programs, the architects created QuickTime digital movies about the cityscape. They pointed cameras out the car window and converted the video capture into digital movies, translating the energy and feel of moving through an environment onto the screen, set, of course, to music recorded on the car radio.

From digitized animations that were no more than 30-second thumbnail sketches, the architects started to visualize spaces by building up and layering planes in different colors and materials. The computer was not used as a rendering tool but as a way of modeling how the eye moved through a rich procession of planes, as though experiencing glimpses of the walls and billboards of the city. The architects were finding the design through a process that mixed time into space. The visualization process started suggesting the angles of the walls, the lighting, alternating blocks of transparency and opacity, and the glow of translucent walls. The digital models encouraged, at the push of a button, the repetition of forms. In feedback loops, the architects added to the movie, incorporating stills into animation clips that were building up a complex digital environment.

With their emphasis on simulating experience, the movies helped the architects construct the space visually before planning it: they built digital stage sets for the work without thinking through the floor plan. With more modeling, a circulation core loosely fell into place, but the plan did not dictate form. The plan was not the generator but a consequence, and an episodic path emerged that left the impression of meandering down the middle of a village. People would bump into each other, and encounter the unexpected on their way to a destination they couldn't see in advance. The visualization was then translated into construction drawings.

The architects had to construct their design in ten weeks, which necessitated using building techniques and materials common in conventional residential construction – Homasote, Lumasite, Gridcore, aluminum channels, Stonco flood lights, raw plywood, Sheetrock, clear-coated concrete floors, and gang-nail, two-by-four trusses, all deployed in unusual ways. Lumasite, traditionally, is used for making signs, but at Fuel the transparent material walled the offices. Instead of using the trusses as roof structure, the architects tilted them up on end within the existing shed. Collectively, the trusses defined a path conceived as an information bar that carried all the infrastructural systems, including ducts, cables and wiring. The architects made liberal use of stay-awake colors, like chartreuse. Producers occupied one side of the bar, and animators, the other, with the circulation in the middle.

ABOVE FUEL. DETAIL SHOWING MATERIAL CONVERGENCE.
MIDDLE GROUND ZERO. PROCESSIONAL RAMP.
RIGHT MINDFIELD. ALUMINUM-CLAD WALL PENETRATING THE ENVELOPE OF THE BUILDING.

The solution was immediate, impermanent, and above all, spirited, and it served the business need of creating a mark within its niche market, acting like a semaphore of professional originality. The design for Fuel was high-octane, smart, original, and in its gritty way, charming. The architects had created a portrait building, one that represented the clients in a way they wanted to be seen.

The 8,000-sq.ft. project at the corner of Pico and Main in Santa Monica was a breakthrough achievement for the firm, and a seminal project in the field, taking creative advantage of the confluences of different design disciplines on the computer screen. Computers were only recently accessible financially to boutique offices interested in exploring the potential of digital design, and Fuel proved an early foray that did not use the computer merely for illustration. The commission opened the way to projects of comparable ambition and originality.

The next exploratory commission that propelled Shubin + Donaldson on the trajectory into original territory was the adaptive reuse of another warehouse for an advertising agency, Ground Zero. The client's brief was telling and compelling: "Blow our minds." But they also wanted their

creative process to be experienced on a promenade through the space, on the "swimming with the fish" principle: an effective ad agency lives with the clients, and the clients reasoned that the working process should reveal itself with transparency from the moment clients enter. They were diving into a fish tank for the swim.

Shubin + Donaldson's solution challenged all the rituals inherent in office design, from the blunt fact of a front lobby controlling access to the conference rooms, to the status of executive offices dominating the working pool from strategic corners. The architectural surgery was radical, and opened up the office to a fresh plan that indeed allowed clients to peer everywhere in the organization, as though looking at a map.

The inescapable reality of Los Angeles urbanism is that it starts with the car and the parking lot. Shubin + Donaldson worked with this given, building a pedestrian ramp from the parking area to the upper level of the building, where the ramp punctures the wall and then descends 150 feet through the center of the space, allowing an overview of the entire floor. The elevated promenade pierces several translucent wall-to-wall, floor-to-ceiling theatrical scrims that both subdivide and mystify the space, landing at the ground floor where a trash can full of awards greets visitors, telling them not to be too impressed. The design ranges from the heroic to the anti-heroic. A row of "war rooms," each dedicated to a current client, lines one side of the space, built with exposed gang-nail steel trusses in scissoring geometries that support glistening walls of ribbed plastic. Glass-topped, kidney-shaped work stations, under swiveling lights that look like street lamps, populate an open plan where the furniture, on wheels, seems ready to go, as though poised at some imaginary starting line. The idea is that the Ground Zero team is ever at the ready, each individual an athlete of creativity.

The architects arrived at this dramatic solution by the incremental steps of a logical decision process. Early digital modeling of the interior produced the idea of layering the space with space divisions hanging from the trusses, but the existing wood trusses could not support any additional load, and walls built up to the tall trusses were prohibitively expensive. Any spatial divisions had to be self-supporting.

To articulate divisions in the cavernous space without building a building within the structure, the architects proposed the idea of scrims arrayed in planes that subdivided the hall. With light falling through skylights, the architects studied the changing effects of natural and artificial light on the

ABOVE OGILVY & MATHER. LAYERING OF MATERIALS AT THE ENTRANCE.

scrims, and how the illuminated scrims modeled the space: the scrims would register shadow and direct light, or they would simply bask in the light and glow. They could also act as light baffles for people who needed limited light. With slow computers affordable at the time, the architects studied different degrees of transparency by allowing the computers to render the images overnight for morning delivery. The transparencies and translucencies that resulted throughout the final design, from scrim to ribbed acrylic planes, are differential, creating the effect of a gossamer fabric bristling with reflections from indeterminate sources. Minimalist without being white, the scrims generated a kind of visual mist that fogs the space. The final effect, so dependent on the luminosity of the scrims, grew from a simple idea visualized on the computer.

Besides being economical, the scrims made a decisive gesture that was straightforward and rational, and emerged within a clean, pure box slashed by the walk, set at an angle to the scrims to heighten the experience of the promenade. Ephemeral in its overall effect, the basic parti was very simple, and the architects kept the strength by distilling the elements to a few essentials, all of which captured light.

Shubin + Donaldson reinvented the wheel in this project, down to the work station, taking nothing off the shelf, avoiding any insinuation of a staid corporate culture that might creep in through products bought off the shelf. The design was less about form than about sensibility.

On a roll after the construction of its new agency, Ground Zero in 2000 secured the 20,000-sq.ft. warehouse next door, commissioning Shubin + Donaldson to design an expansion for its post-production facilities, Mindfield. The architects continued to design on the computer, but decided to use a 3-D modeling program, Form Z, to shape the space, testing computer images with constructed maquettes in what emerged as a hybrid back-and-forth process of digital and physical modeling. Under the influence of Form Z, the architects produced the most spatially complex of their projects to date.

The warehouse was another bow-truss structure allowing an open-plan work space. The clients had just returned from Bilbao and a visit to the Guggenheim, and they brought with them their enthusiasm for its piscine shapes, importing the curving language to the orthogonal layout of the existing structure. The afterimage of Bilbao, which, contrary to expectations, was composed primarily of Richard Serra's Torqued Ellipses rather than Frank Gehry's masterpiece, sent the design in a direction the architects had not employed in previous projects, but it did confirm their pattern of accommodating the tastes and requirements of successive clients, and even the same client in successive projects: language for the architects comes out of the specifics of each commission and not from any formal branding of their own.

The clients who had previously asked the architects to "blow their minds," pushed the architects into new territory when they suggested that form does not have to follow function, that function could follow form. Set in motion, the arcing aluminum-clad walls careened through the space, one structure playing through another in dynamic, tilting combinations. The contractors simply set up jigs, and quickly and efficiently built the curved shapes, which were non-structural.

Curvilinear forms became a different way of organizing the space, giving the architects a vectorial understanding of spatial organization, and affecting how the architects ushered visitors into and through the building dynamically. The architects collided and intersected arcs, creating at the intersections, by spontaneous generation, rooms and spaces that never would have resulted from a more conventional design process. Sweeping curves intersected walls with exposed steel studs in a normally taboo juxtaposition of the plastic and tectonic, the sculptural and structural. At the leading edge of the structure, a piece of the curving wall that escaped the perimeter becomes the signature of the design and a visual logo of the company. The company was breaking out of the box and breaking out of convention.

Many institutions, like the Guggenheim in New York, are defined in the public mind by the buildings they occupy, and perhaps no business is more susceptible to a consciousness about image and self-image than an ad agency. Ogilvy, the advertising giant, contacted Shubin + Donaldson because by 2000, the architects had become masters in the delicate matter of repositioning a company through design: the architects could deliver a complete make-over, from work space to attitude. Ogilvy, long a fixture of a corporate address and an exponent of a button-down corporate mentality, had decided to facilitate a renaissance of business and clientele in times that had deeply shifted by changing the culture of the company. It was a business rather than a style decision, but one in which style amounted to business.

The executives decided to perform surgery on the company's image while changing venue from offices in a Wilshire high-rise to a warehouse in a Culver City complex, Conjunctive Points, designed by Eric Owen Moss. Ogilvy was effectively rebranding itself, and architecture was the highly visible vehicle. Ogilvy pointedly did not seek out a corporate design firm but one specialized in the alternative design of an avant-garde studio. The "office lift" also meant social engineering via a floor plan that encouraged freer flows of thinking. In the former space on Wilshire, in the context of a plan that reified the lines of authority of the office, the creative directors occupied privatized offices, and were not out in the open, in the center, on a frequented back-and-forth path. The plan itself worked against the bump-up of ideas in chance encounters. With this kind of plan, colleagues met by appointment.

The architect's reinterpretation of the company started at the door, with the plan. The long ramp at Ground Zero from the parking lot to the trash can had established an almost ceremonial transition into an interior realm. Shubin + Donaldson, in a new context, transformed the idea by creating a long walk-through culvert, a tube, its armature of Unistrut steel ribs sheathed in perforated aluminum sheets. It was a different morphology, but it performed the same function as a transition into an interior world that it brought into focus. Like Alice's looking glass, the tube acted as a psychological passageway to a special world beyond.

The architects, as always, were masters at modulating light, but here of necessity, to control it for people working at computer screens. Instead of throttling down the apertures by closing walls, the architects filtered the light by layering variously translucent materials, like perforated aluminum, Lumasite, Plexiglas panels, and Thermoclear, which all control daylight in different ways. The umbilical tube itself, large-scale and dramatic, serves as the primary light filter, like a canopy of leaves in a forest, for the broad expanses of glass façade facing the eastern sun. At night, the collage of light-catching materials transforms light into points, blurs, and streaks, creating an environment of pixelated effects. Never does the eye see the light source, just the secondary effects materialized in the transparent and translucent collage. The same light works through the layers, multiplied. Passage through the space, especially in the umbilical tube, seems like walking into and through a kaleidoscopic tunnel.

The architects placed uplights on the tops of trusses to bounce off the warm, sandblasted wood ceiling, and to reveal the vaulted volume of the roof at night: the wood warms and softens the light. Translucent materials capture light in ways that also reveal form in space: what seems transparent and ephemeral in some lights shifts to volumetric solidity in others. As in other warehouse projects, such as Fuel and Ground Zero, the time frame for building out the space was compressed, allowing only a few months for design and not much more for construction. There was no time to overwork the design, and great pressure in favor of simple construction systems and big, generous gestures. The materials had to be immediately and locally available, to reduce lead time.

If, for creative agencies, the corporate formalities of Wilshire Boulevard became the cultural paradigm not to follow, it is an ironic turnaround that the kind of aesthetic and spirit that effloresced in the iconoclastic warehouses designed by Shubin + Donaldson rebounded to the office spaces of Wilshire, the margins overtaking the mainstream. The tidy little secret of steel-and-glass high-rises, with their built-to-impress marble-clad lobbies, is that they are basically loft buildings that can accommodate cavernous, free-wheeling designs. The standard open plan of these spaces also means open volume.

Soon after completing Ogilvy, Shubin + Donaldson did several of these conversions, importing design attitudes the firm had cultivated in LA's warehouse districts to the city's most corporate avenue. Ogilvy needn't have moved.

One of these was the complete remake of a former bank on the ground floor of a building on Wilshire, in Beverly Hills, into offices for The Firm, a talent management agency. The architects started by subtraction, stripping away any traces of the polished materials that previously belonged to the bank. The marble around the columns was the first material to go, along with the carpets and the dropped ceiling. The architects stripped the space down to its raw shell, revealing the basic concrete structure and its textured patina. There was energy in the rawness.

The architects then judiciously added elements, but nothing more polished than painted sheet rock and storefront façades with exposed metal clips holding the glass. Office cubicles were walled-in acrylic panels supported by simple frames of raw steel. Desks and low partitions in the central space serving perimeter offices were built from low-cost medium density fiberboard (MDF), which was sealed but not painted. The architects clear-coated the concrete floor, leaving all the irregularities and blemishes. The only luxury was an occasional high-tech stainless-steel fitting, the brushed-aluminum receptionist desk, warm slatted-wood ceilings in the conference room, and the sheer luminosity throughout: the architects again treated light as a primary material. They spot-lit the columns, uplit the ceiling, and treated the offices lining the perimeter of the space as a backlit glass scrim forming a light wall. They also backlit the translucent glass railing at the mezzanine. Glow itself formed a large part of the material collage.

The design versatility that architects bring to warehouse conversions for LA's creative industries ranges widely, and Shubin + Donaldson Architects carry over the same attitude of adapting to the particulars of each commission in the company's residential projects: they remain portrait architects, designing in the image of the commission rather than with a portable signature. The architects do not transport a vocabulary of forms from job to job: what they bring is an attitude about the necessity of invention.

The basis of their residential commissions is inherently more conservative from a design point of view than that for creative agencies, not only because of the environmental spur necessary in talent businesses, but also because of the entire apparatus of home ownership – from home-lending practice to resale value and domestic expectations. When the client who had commissioned the headquarters for Fuel, for example, asked the architects to remodel his beach house in Malibu, on a tight site on the Pacific Coast Highway, he wanted the house to be an urban retreat, with a spa-like environment. He didn't want to recreate at home the energy of his workplace, but asked instead for the opposite, a place to relax. Instead of playing the design for edge, the architects played it toward serenity. They specified limestone, natural woods, and translucent glass instead of inexpensive industrial materials like Lumasite and concrete.

If, in their warehouses, the architects generate raw visual energy and infuse the environment with edge, in their homes, edge gives way to serenity as they pursue architectural beauty of a different, more conventionally Modernist nature. Still, architecture is the art of the possible, and the architects seize the moment even in residential commissions when they feel they can push into new territory.

In a house they designed for art collectors in Montecito, the architects carried over a certain temperament from their warehouses, creating a loft-like environment in a structure made inexpensively from the ground up with industrial systems and materials. The architects wrapped a motor court with tall mute walls surfaced in stucco and centered on an abstract, interlocking entry composed of steel, translucent glass and granite. Beyond, the architects created a long three-bedroom structure under a shed metal roof organized along a spine open to plate-glass views at either end.

Spaces are lofty, the volumes tall, and the architects created long runs of wall space for paintings. There is nothing fussy about the detailing, other than the engineering gadgetry of the off-the-shelf steel trusses holding up the ribbed steel roof. In an otherwise plain but generous building, they confirm the ethos of modernity with special moments and pieces. Besides the sculptural entry, there is a standard, industrial fireplace with a steel flue, which they encase in fire-etched tempered glass planes, a composition that announces, in a

ABOVE ARTIST STUDIO. DETAIL SHOWING THE MATERIAL PALETTE OF LUMASITE, GLASS, CONCRETE, AND CEDAR SHINGLES.

central and pivotal moment, the contemporary spirit of the house design.

The most spirited of their houses, the one that directly translates the strategies and attitudes of their warehouse designs into the suburbs, is an art studio in Santa Barbara. On a eucalyptus-studded site overlooking the ocean, the architects essentially established from the ground up, the premise of a warehouse, by creating a voluminous shed-like structure, roofed with an off-center wood truss leaning against a two-story tall shingled wall. The side opposite is enclosed by wood trusses standing on end and sheathed with ribbed acrylic panels. Within the framework of this volume, open at the front to the view, the architects nested an independent glass-and-stucco structure programmed as a guest house on the ground floor and an open painting studio above. The ceiling of the studio is surfaced in strand board, and the floor, covered in plywood deck subfloor, is left natural. The structure cost less than $200/sq.ft., and was made of the most conventional, garden-variety materials chosen for their raw vitality and their ability to enclose big volumes cheaply. The result is a highly sculpted, spatially and materially complex structure that holds its heroic own in this big landscape.

Not since Frank Gehry's house in Santa Monica has there been a California house done with such freshness, directness, and energy. Again, the house passes the test of appropriateness for the clients and the site. But it is as unexpected as any of the warehouse innovations that were, in their contexts, so innovative. The architects brought to this Santa Barbara commission, in a community that often verges on a narcissistic comfort architecture, the vitality, curiosity, and virtuosity they exhibit in town in their most challenging commissions. With their open process, which accepts the specifics of each commission, they are not importing signature forms that they already know, but bringing to their commissions an attitude about creativity and exploration that makes their environments surprisingly fresh. Their originality is that their designs are not so much about form but about the hard-to-define, difficult-to-capture issue of attitude.

FORM FOLLOWS INTENTION
INTERVIEWS WITH SHUBIN + DONALDSON

GROUND ZERO

ADVERTISING AGENCY / 6-17
INTERVIEW WITH JIM SMITH, CLIENT

SHUBIN
We got this project because one of the employees from Ground Zero had been going to parties at Fuel. A lot of these companies place real value on the importance of hanging out (laughs), and networking within their design community, and ultimately their spaces acquiesce to good parties. I remember the first meeting that we had with Jim and his partners; they admitted up front that the ideas in the design needed to be the most crucial factor and that all other considerations should fall out of that. It wasn't a secret that there was no real budget, but they leveraged risk taking and total creative freedom against that. That's our ilk. That's a good client for us.

SMITH
This was an unusual journey for us to embark on, because as an entity that prides itself on being a creative business we were giving up control to another entity whose charge was to do something creative. I don't think many people know how to be inventive in an environment where the client believes that they are the visionaries, and still work perfectly well together.

DONALDSON
This relationship prompted a lot of compelling questions: How do you help a company establish itself? How can the space help do that? It really hinged on an attitude, and for Ground Zero it was a non-hierarchical attitude.

SMITH
It was always a creative mission to see if we could have an environment that was reflective of us, rather than one that simply served our needs. We're a company that likes you to be immersed right in the middle, immediately, and we're unafraid of that.

DONALDSON
We made them an unreasonable proposal: run a ramp up a full story in height outside the length of the building, cut a hole in the wall, and run the ramp back down a full story again through the length of the space. Everyone has to walk through the entire space before getting to the receptionist. No one gets off the ramp without making that journey.

SHUBIN
Remember, this is an idea driven client, so they got it. They understood that the strategy needed to be uncompromising. It's like the experience of going up a freeway onramp. You know you're going up and you're anticipating that something is going to happen. Also by entering the building above the ground, it shifts the perspective of how you experience the space.

SMITH
We were quite keen on having something that was not over-designed. The scheme is obviously a design element, but it doesn't hammer you over the head all the way down the ramp. I don't think the building looks inadequate because it's raw. It just doesn't look like we disappeared up our own ass in an ever decreasing debate about where to put the light sockets.

SHUBIN
Yeah, (laughs) I think the priorities are clearly communicated in the design. The broad stroke, the concept, the important strategic decisions, are what really speak. I always thought that that was consistent with how you guys approached your business.

SMITH
Architecture, as commerce, is as old as when the first nobles started commissioning the first painters or sculptors or musicians to do something for them in their cold windy castles. The good ones would probably say to the king, "Can you tell me why you want that large tapestry, or what you would like it to say." And kings, like clients, were probably not always able to give the artist a good articulation of that. So it was up to the skill of the tapestry maker, or the painter, or the harpsichordist to figure it out, and to have a go at doing it. It doesn't ever change much. It doesn't change in our business. Your skill, if you like, is your ability to really understand the client's vision even when the client is perhaps not the best at articulating it, and then apply your own creative vision in a way that makes it compatible.

DONALDSON
Our strongest work is usually the result of a good match between our skills and the client's, and how they interact. At times, I almost thought of us as a branch of Ground Zero.

SMITH
Yeah, I've always thought of it that way as well. If we had had an architectural facet to Ground Zero, we might have designed something like what you did for us. For me, your business is overwhelmingly a creative business; it isn't what I would call a functional business. You're like us. You're the kind of company for the contrarian, because you're out on that edge. But what also made it work was that you're very good listeners. You can't get there just with genius if you're not a good listener. We've ended up in a few of the wrong places even though we think we're geniuses, because we weren't listening, not because we weren't creative. Whenever we do something bad, it isn't because we got uncreative, it's because we got deaf.

DONALDSON

We have a genuine interest in our clients. Some are closer to the core of our ideals and some are farther away, but at the end of the day we do try to listen. We also try to listen to what people are really trying to do, not just what they want. Sometimes clients will come to us and say they need a cool conference room, but we want to know why they need a cool conference room. So there's the importance of listening, but you also have to be able to ask a decent question, because they're as important as anything else.

SHUBIN

After we all got clear and agreed on a set of design intentions, we started to model the shell of the building in the computer so that we could study it.

DONALDSON

And we hung a series of transparent scrims in the computer model. We let it render overnight, and came back in the morning to see these surfaces stacked up on each other, making a kind of fog in the space. The scrims were able to tame the size of the warehouse and they transformed the space into a kind of landscape. I'd had Robert Irwin's scrim pieces on my mind, which I had seen as a student in Italy at the Villa Panza in Varese. I'd always loved their clarity and resourcefulness. You would walk into a room and what you thought was a wall turned out to be a stretched piece of fabric.

SHUBIN

We were also interested in certain things going on in artistic culture. The work of Bill Viola, and the idea of projecting imagery in space had real potency. The internet was also just coming along, and we started to develop an interest in the relationships between built space and companies' virtual internet presence. As you travel on the ramp, you're in this alternating current of observation and immersion with the inner workings of the company. You're moving over this sea of desks, and through these scrims which often had Ground Zero's work projected onto them. The scrims were like an aurora borealis in the space that exhibited natural and technological phenomena.

SMITH

I remember that we didn't have, according to conventional measures, the kind of money needed to build out a space of that size, to accommodate the number of people we had, and to put in the kind of programming that we were talking about. We decided that you were going to have to figure it out. In the end the building doesn't look cheap, but it also doesn't look like we wasted money on it. There's a subtle distinction there. When we do advertising, we create without thinking about the budget, in fact we assume that there isn't one. And what tends to happen is that ideas come out that are simple and pure. The building is a mirror image of that. The building is a very simple idea. It was an unbelievably complex thing to execute, but when you're in it you don't have to do a lot of thinking about what's going on there.

SHUBIN

We gathered materials that were easily accessible and started figuring out how to put them together and craft them. Even though we had been experimenting with process in the computer, we were also interested in material research and development, on all of the elements including the work stations.

DONALDSON

We really had to pare down the language of the materials to a handful of things. There were steel studs, Thermoclear plastic, and glass, a pre-engineered mezzanine system, the scrims, and a little bit of sheet rock and paint. And it was all erectable by carpenters so we kept the trades to a minimum. We needed fast assembly and took the budget and ridiculously short construction schedule seriously.

SMITH

You know I had a wander around the building the other day and years later it still works in all of the ways that we intended. That's a pretty interesting thing to be able to pull off. If we're honest, once you get into the building it's a whole different matter. If you go back through recorded history all the great pieces of art are done by evil fascist dictators, aren't they? Great pieces of art are not designed by the Bill Clintons of the world; they're done by the Machiavellis. Once you move into a building democracy takes over and you end up with dodgy little potted plants all over the bloody place. It drives me crazy, but I'm still uncompromising about what that space should communicate.

ABOVE LOS ANGELES FREEWAY IN THE MIST. GETTY IMAGES.

MINDFIELD

POST-PRODUCTION / 18-25
INTERVIEW WITH JIM SMITH, CLIENT

SHUBIN
A year later after finishing Ground Zero, Jim acquired the building next door and he wanted to put the post-production wing of his company in there. So we started to entertain ideas of how we might make connections between the two buildings. We worked on a number of strategies. We looked at a bridge that would drop down into a outdoor space on the Mindfield side. We also looked at excavating the ground in Mindfield and then ramping the entire floor down, almost like a quarry.

SMITH
This was also around the time that I went to Bilbao to see the Guggenheim, and I was quite keen on the idea of trying to translate some of my experiences into this project.

DONALDSON
Jim was excited about Bilbao, and so were we, but our interests had less to do with the actual structure. We were really taken by Richard Serra's Tilted Arcs. We were interested in their scale and method of fabrication. Serra has these plates made to specification at a shipyard and he doesn't polish or paint them. They're left as is. Because of their associations with heavy industry and their leviathan qualities they carry a sense of anonymity. They don't have an overwhelming sense of authorship. This lack of authorship has been part of our attitude. We haven't been interested in a signature style, but I do think that we have a signature attitude or process. A lot of our interests tend to hover around issues of scale and monumentality: civil engineering projects, infrastructure, the aerospace and film industries; but also in terms of natural phenomena: the ocean, deserts, mountains, the scope of viewing landscape from the sky, the panoramic device. These are interests that are particular to the West, and their anonymity is attractive to us. This interest in monumentality is clear in our commercial work, but it also exists in a lot of our residential work as well. So we'll often conceptualize a project with language from those worlds... excavation, carving, bridging, mass, ballast...

SHUBIN
The strategy for this project was a coalescing between our influences from Serra's sculpture and a genetic relationship with aspects of the design from Ground Zero.

DONALDSON
The conference room of Ground Zero provided the DNA for the circulation spine in Mindfield. It's a corridor of trusses that march through the entire length of the building, and cut through spaces indiscriminately.

SHUBIN
The progression of the circulation spine through the building is continuously intersected by a series of arcing aluminum walls that weave throughout the floor plan. And when these rational and irrational parts of the project meet they create all kinds of unanticipated residual spaces that are eccentric and sculptural and were programmed as meeting rooms, bathrooms, the kitchen and eating areas, and offices.

SMITH
Those odd-shaped spaces are tremendously attractive places for people to be in. Where no two planes run in the same direction, and those curved walls bounce light so you have a mix of artificial and natural light. You can't legislate for little bits of genius cropping up like that.

SHUBIN
This was definitely a case of 'function follows form'. The space does have great functionality, but function can be found intuitively, and it can exist in sculptural form. The truth of the matter is that process is rarely linear, and even though we look at programming very rigorously it can't get you there by itself.

DONALDSON
We wanted an undeniable signifier at the entrance; something that was brazen and permanent. So we carved out the corner of the building, pulled back the skin of the existing shell and let the arc crash through it.

ABOVE RICHARD SERRA. INSTALLATION VIEW OF TORQUED ELLIPSES AT THE DIA BEACON. BEACON, NY. PHOTO COURTESY HEATHER PETERSON.

MONTECITO RESIDENCE
26-31

SHUBIN
Originally the clients were going to add on and renovate their home, and basically on a napkin sketch we convinced them that if we looked at alternative ways of making form and structure they might be able to build a new house.

DONALDSON
We were working against a tight budget and we wanted to try and get as much architecture out of it as possible. So we decided to borrow from the commercial construction world by using Vulcraft trusses, steel pan deck, and basic warehouse technology. The clients knew our commercial work, and were comfortable with having us do their home but they didn't want it to look like one of our interior projects. We thought of the house as a suburban loft to house their art. They have a beautiful collection of Southern California artists, Sam Francis, Chuck Arnoldi, as well as other contemporaries, like Sean Scully and Alex Katz. We wanted to get the house to hold their art properly.

SHUBIN
And at the time it was also unusual for a contemporary home to be built in Montecito, normally it's a traditional enclave.

DONALDSON
This house was influenced quite a bit by my experience working on the Crawford House, back when I worked for Morphosis. The Crawford House was really a kind of precedent, because it's also in Montecito, and we actually used the same builder, Paul Franz. There was an attitude that carried over, and you can see it in the use of steel, the repetition of structural elements; in fact the material palettes are quite similar. So this house knows who its neighbors are.

SHUBIN
We wanted to modulate and control the experience of the site, with opportunities to experience some aspect of it from each room. The perception of horizon lines, whether in a horizontal landscape view or vertical portrait view, informed the architecture. The exterior of this house is like a fortress with solid mass walls and a steel column jutting out of the entry piece. The thick bearing-wall tradition of Santa Barbara is set against a warehouse aesthetic normally found in Los Angeles. Even though it is a modern house, it has the attitude and organization of the original Spanish houses.

DONALDSON
In Santa Barbara there is a tradition of entry courts that goes back to George Washington Smith and the Spanish haciendas. Generally there are very few windows on the public façade. But once you go into the house, it opens up to gardens and courtyards. That sequence of hiding and revealing is something that we're really interested in, and it has cropped up in other work of ours.

ABOVE MORPHOSIS. CRAWFORD RESIDENCE. SANTA BARBARA, CA. 1988. PHOTO COURTESY KIM ZWARTS.

URBAN SPA

38-45
INTERVIEW WITH SETH EPSTEIN, CLIENT

SHUBIN

Seth came to us with a fully developed narrative about the kinds of experiences that he wanted to have living here. We would talk about how architecture can cause you to live a certain way; how it can call you to action or back you into doing something.

EPSTEIN

We knew what kinds of experiences that we wanted the house to make possible for us. Beach houses are very sensuous, visceral places where you are attuned to ranges in texture, light, and temperature.

DONALDSON

On any given site there are natural conditions and situations that already exist which you can harness and use almost like materials. A house can be designed to modulate with the seasons and climate. It doesn't have to be a static object. Transition and transformation were ideas that we really explored. We thought that the house should liberate you from the density and chaos of living along the highway in Malibu. Once you crossed though the front door threshold all of that was meant to fall away. The house was also meant to act as a mediation between the harshness of the Pacific Coast Highway and the natural environment of the ocean; a gradient between the extremities of the man-made and the natural environment.

SHUBIN

We wanted the house to be open and intimate and to have a lot of visual connection to the ocean, but Malibu is a very public place. Apart from the constant stream of cars along PCH, you also have people on the beach most of the time. So we had to be very strategic about how we established relationships between the interior and environment. You can see the ocean from almost every room, and it draws you through the house without relinquishing any privacy. The transitions between the bathroom, bedroom, and outdoor spaces were meant to be seamless, and the idea of the spa really centered around the master suite. The bathroom and dressing area were intentionally thought of as social space, almost like a five star luxury spa suite nested within a private home. The clients could spend time relaxing with their friends in this part of the house, rather than going to the spa at the Four Seasons or driving out to Palm Springs for the weekend.

DONALDSON

A lot of this focus on the master bath came out of the tradition of bathing culture on the West Coast. It's like an updated version of people in the early 20th century going to mineral springs in the mountains to rejuvenate themselves, or the eastern tradition of Japanese bath houses.

EPSTEIN

Functionally, the bathroom was incredible. The glass wall with mirrors that floated in space was genius because it produced natural, soft-box lighting. There was a soothing quality to the glass in contrast to the heat outside. And there were three translucent sliding panels that opened into the bedroom so that you could choose the level of privacy that you wanted.

SHUBIN

The limestone and the dark wenge wood had a texture and solidness that weighed against the lightness and subtlety of the translucent glass. We designed the vanity, the tub, and the cabinetry to feel like pieces of furniture which emphasized the sense of the bath as a room that you could relax and rejuvenate in.

ABOVE CANVAS BEACH CABANA.

BRAND NEW SCHOOL

MOTION GRAPHICS / 46-51

DONALDSON

This is a little bit of a departure from some of our other commercial spaces, in terms of tone. It almost has the qualities of a Shaker meeting house: the symmetry, the spare surfaces with close attention to detail and craft, as well as the presence of a rigorous work ethic.

SHUBIN

The owner, Jonathan Notaro, bases his design approach on the grid. He wanted the precision of his thinking to be conveyed in the design, but he didn't want the architecture to overshadow their work, so we created an infrastructure for them to design within. There's an intentional layout of spatial relationships with two monolithic bars on either side to accommodate the designers and producers. And in the middle there is an area for collaboration, which has a softer expression. That organization is clear when you look down on it from above. From the mezzanine you can read the formal manifestation of Brand New School's collaborative process.

DONALDSON

Up there you can also grasp that this is really a building within a building. It almost looks like this intact piece of infrastructure that was slid in through the hangar door.

SHUBIN

We felt if you're paying for a warehouse space, and you don't get a chance to experience all of that volume, then you're not leveraging what your experience of the space could be.

DONALDSON

Even though this is clearly an industrial space, it has taken on some domestic functions. It sort of has one foot in the residential world, and one in the commercial. In the past 10 years we have seen an interest in domesticating the office. Parts of an office that were once fairly marginalized, are now some of things that we work on very closely... kitchens, lounges, outdoor spaces. I think creative companies have realized that people are often more conducive to creative activity when they are in a comfortable environment or one which inspires them to think and make, and these are often domestic spaces. There has also been a fundamental shift in lifestyle. Many people are beginning to live and work the way artists and writers always have, and they are making choices about their living and working environments that facilitate a creative lifestyle.

SHUBIN

We have an adage in the office that we call "working at home and homing at work." That's precisely what Robin is talking about. This building is located in a commercial complex with galleries, artist studios, and other creative office spaces. There are probably a fair amount of creative businesses here making work "at the kitchen table," and artists going to sleep at night in their airplane hangars.

ABOVE JAMES TURRELL. LUNETTE. 1974. INSTALLATION AT THE VILLA PANZA. VARESE, ITALY. PHOTO COURTESY ROBIN DONALDSON.

WONG DOODY
ADVERTISING AGENCY / 52-59

SHUBIN
When we do adaptive reuse projects in warehouse spaces like this we typically cannot touch the building. So we think of them as a chassis or an envelope to design within. These spaces have beautiful layers of decay and fragments left over from their past uses and urban memories. The misregistration that can happen when you put a creative office into a fruit packing warehouse, or in this case a beer shipping facility, creates all kinds of eccentricites that people are very drawn to.

DONALDSON
This idea of misregistration is another form of the irrationality or unreasonableness that we've talked about in other projects; like the ramp in Ground Zero or the tube in Ogilvy. They set up experiences that you would never have arrived at by methodological analysis. They're generated through forms of intuition, perception, and memory, and yet they function very well. This is why a firehouse can end up being a great location for a restaurant, or why so many art museums can slip so easily into factory buildings.

SHUBIN
In Wong Doody, there were huge zinc doors with graphic remnants left over from the shipping days that we wanted to incorporate in some way. These doors which used to demarcate large refrigerated sections of the building were kept and used in various ways. One became a large magnetic surface for posting work, another remained functional and when open could double the size of the main conference room, others became elements for dividing up space. We were interested in the idea of the old meeting the new, the raw meeting the refined. Because we couldn't touch the shell of the building we had to develop a strategy for the space that could abide by that. So we devised a series of meeting rooms that were inserted into the center of the space.

DONALDSON
They're like a village of temporary architectures; pavilions, that are each clad in a distinct material: cork, black and green chalkboard, and silver dry-erase. Usually these kinds of materials are thought of as thin applied surfaces, but here they feel volumetric. The blackboard surfaces have the visual weight and inertia of blocks of stone. These surfaces are also interactive and changing. The chalkboards and dry-erase are like palimpsests of images and messages. Work in progress gets pinned up on the cork.

SHUBIN
We also used the location of the existing skylights to inform and shape the layout of the space. We studied how light moves through the building during the day, and choreographed programmatic elements around that. We tried to treat light as a three-dimensional material, which we thought of in

programmatic elements around that. We tried to treat light as a three-dimensional material, which we thought of in terms of carving and sculpting.

DONALDSON
The idea was that you'd 'read' the light, in shafts or shapes; that it would have geometry.

ABOVE JAMES TURRELL. SKY SPACE. INSTALLATION AT THE VILLA PANZA. VARESE, ITALY. PHOTO COURTESY ROBIN DONALDSON.

RIVIERA RESIDENCE

60-71

DONALDSON

I've always felt that this house is related to the Santa Barbara Estate. It has similar articulations of materiality, proportion, and massing. Even though this house is modest in size it still appears impressive, because of the way it takes advantage of its site. Perched on the top of a ridge overlooking Santa Barbara, it is situated in a way that the expansive views framed by the house interlace with the architecture. The front elevation's apparent sense of significant scale also comes from the pairing of monolithic wall planes and transparent surfaces.

SHUBIN

The monumentality of this house is created by perceived space. By capturing these views and taking advantage of opportunities for more integrated living with the outdoors, the house appears to be much larger than it actually is. These perceptions have sustainable implications. You can increase the livable area of your house by further engagement with the natural environment, while reducing the carbon footprint of the building.

DONALDSON

The relationship of the house to its context is fairly complex. It has to do with how the clients, and ourselves, regard the stewardship of the land. For all of us, it was important to create a sense of place and to build something that had real integrity. Most great places in the world are the product of a belief system, and we wanted to create something that would be lasting and have as little impact on the environment as possible.

SHUBIN

We didn't tear up a pristine chunk of hillside. We used the existing foundation and recycled whatever materials we could. The existing house was taken apart piece-by-piece and all of the usable components were donated to Habitat for Humanity. But sustainability goes beyond using photovoltaics, heat capture, and radiant heat floors; although those are also important elements in this house. In our minds sustainable issues are not exclusive to technologies. Natural systems such as siting, view sheds, solar orientation, and so on, need to be addressed as a first order. You don't have to make a display of your sustainable systems and devices unless that is your intention, and aesthetics certainly do not have to be determined by them.

DONALDSON

In fact, the answer is not always technology. In some ways technology got the industrial world into a mess and more of it is not necessarily going to get us out. Sustainability can be found in so many forms. Your average gothic cathedral is the ultimate sustainable building. It supported a local economy for hundreds of years while it was being constructed. It was made from stone that came from a local quarry, and could be taken apart and rebuilt into another structure if need be. And five hundred years later it still serves as a religious space and adds beauty and significance to a community. Apart from a little frankincense now and then, it's not spewing anything into the atmosphere. That's a sustainable model that makes sense to us. It has to do with beauty, community, physical integrity, the sourcing of local labor and materials, and endurance.

SHUBIN

How sustainable is a house if you tear it down in fifteen years, or even in fifty? The conversation between architecture and the environment is crucial, but we shouldn't overlook the importance of the relationship between buildings and culture. The cultural foothold can have a lot of bearing on the longevity and cultural value of a building.

DONALDSON

People are going to have to consider stewardship and sense of place over real estate investments, and look at the possibility of building smaller, higher quality, more lasting, and aesthetically rich homes. I'm comfortable with that as a future direction in our work.

ABOVE MONOLITHIC MASSING. SANTA BARBARA ESTATE. SANTA BARBARA, CA. 2003. PHOTO COURTESY CIRO COELHO.

DUBAI VILLAS
80-89

SHUBIN
The Dubai Villas are the next step in the line of thinking that came out of projects like the Santa Barbara Estate and Bentley. They are all variations on the courtyard typology, and although the climate is obviously more extreme in the UAE, all these projects are situated in an arid to semi-arid climate.

DONALDSON
Our designs are interpretations of a typology and vernacular that has worked well in those arid conditions, and that is part of the reason why they look like they could be relevant in the UAE, Santa Monica, or Scottsdale, Arizona. The Case Study projects are also a significant frame of reference, as they were on the Bentley Residence, Greentree, and the Riviera Residence.

SHUBIN
They are all organized in similar ways, with courtyards and transparency between the interior and exterior. Many of the Case Study projects also had that monolithic impenetrable looking front façade; which arguably is a contemporary interpretation of the Moorish courtyard typology.

DONALDSON
I'm almost embarrassed to admit to the Case Study inflection in these projects, but as born and bred Southern California architects, it just seems to be lodged in our design DNA. And the client wants our West Coast attitude. Part of the reason that they chose us to design these projects, was because they wanted to appropriate that "So Cal" lifestyle and aesthetic.

SHUBIN
That's true. They want the look and feel of the Southern California lifestyle. I think part of that is the Hollywood glamour and luxury image. These projects are formal houses. They have grand entrances, and they are overt demonstrations of wealth and power. They are statement houses, and in that regard they were pretty fun to design. Whether they ever materialize is another issue, but despite the current recessive economy, Statement Homes will continue to be pursued. The world still aspires. There will always be wealthy people who want houses of this magnitude.

DONALDSON
But this rampant expression of capitalistic excessiveness is not exactly a full contradiction, but maybe a partial one from the work we have been doing. It was a distinct departure from the efficiency of many of our other Southern California located custom homes. Despite the relatively modest sizes of the So Cal homes they are actually pretty darn efficient. There is usually a lot of program packed into them. And then to go to Dubai and suddenly be designing very large homes and spaces, and being encouraged to do so, was actually a little odd. And we got to stretch ourselves a bit. However, ultimately I think this particular trajectory of our work has reached its zenith with these designs. Mediterranean courtyard-influenced homes are great, but the big boxy forms clad in stone and plaster, these have kind of run their course for us; at least in terms of the formal language and expression. You cannot take it much further than we did with these Dubai designs.

SHUBIN
Yeah, I think we are on to new things.

DONALDSON
We used this project to introduce BIM (building information modeling) software into the office and found that we could stretch our design vocabulary and our ability to quickly visualize and model, while still keeping the essence of our design values, which are timeless.

SHUBIN
I thought one of the most important things that the office gained from working on these projects was the acquisition of new tools that can move us into other realms; that can push us into new design trajectories. The office also had to function in a way that was not typical for us. We had a fairly constant progression of design charrettes with a larger group of people than are typically involved in a single project. We developed many iterations of each configuration on a pretty aggressive schedule.

DONALDSON
It was also a way of gaining closure on a chapter of our work. And what comes next ? Well I think there will certainly be a shift in our building systems and material palette. I think we are done with drywall and plaster. It is so ubiquitous and we have done so many projects in it, that I think we need to explore other options.

SHUBIN
That's why I am excited about projects like the Toro Canyon Residence. We may still pursue certain archetypal interests like monumentality, but in different terms. In that case the house is literally monolithic; designed entirely in poured in place concrete.

DONALDSON
So there is a new material future for us, and there are also a lot of technologies that have evolved recently in terms of how you clad and waterproof buildings; different skins, materials, and rain screens, and how they affect the building's performance in environmental terms.

SHUBIN

I also think that we will probably find ourselves working on smaller homes with more components. I think people are going to get interested in down-sizing, and in living in homes that are more program efficient. Quality will be more important than quantity.

TOP EARLY STUDY SKETCH. ROBIN DONALDSON.
BOTTOM EARLY STUDY RENDERING. COURTESY SHUBIN + DONALDSON ARCHITECTS.

EAST CHANNEL RESIDENCE

90-95
INTERVIEW WITH JOHN & DEBBIE WARFEL, CLIENTS

DONALDSON
It is important to us that a green home can be both a beautiful design and have rigorous environmental aspirations, and that you don't have to make a compromise on either front. We have a few projects, like the Riviera Residence, that are beautiful high-design homes, but are very green and resource efficient in terms of how they operate. For a while it seemed like the thinking was that good design and green thinking were exclusive and if you were going to have a "green home" it had to have this Rocky Mountain Institute aesthetic with Trombe walls and the whole bit. But your house has a kind of design potential that could be followed, almost as a template. You may have a lifestyle that's a bit less distracted than your average American, but the house is a manifestation of your philosophy about how you live, and the relationship that you have to your environment.

JOHN WARFEL
In all honesty, some of these potentials were achievable because of our lifestyle. We're not gadget people and we don't have many appliances or electronics, in fact we only have one television! The photovoltaic electrical system is producing more than was expected; certainly more than the DWP calculated that it would.

DEBBIE WARFEL
It's generating more electricity than we can use.

DONALDSON
I remember discussions when the house was being laid out, about positioning the house on the site so that it can allow these systems, both natural and technological, to respond to the environment and to perform properly.

DEBBIE WARFEL
Well, you absolutely captured that with the design. One of the advantages we had, and I would certainly insist on it again, is that we lived at the site for a couple of years before we started the design work. We had lived in the canyon, so we knew a lot about that microclimate, but we also learned a lot about the site. It is one thing to know that there is a prevailing breeze in the canyon, but it's another thing to live through a couple of seasons and see what the actual effects of the sun are on the site, and learn that the breezes come up at a very specific time. We decided not to have air conditioning. We built the house on purpose without it. There are usually a few days a year when it would be nice to have, but it's not necessary because the house is three blocks from the beach and is able to capture these prevailing winds.

SHUBIN
Philosophically the house is sort of pre-industrial in terms of its attitude. You could say that prior to the industrial revolution almost all residential architecture was essentially sustainable.

JOHN WARFEL
Absolutely. The solar system for this house is a very high-tech piece of design and philosophy, but solar water heating is thousands of years old. Opening doors to cool the house off is necessary. The house doesn't function on automatic. The air conditioning doesn't just kick in, but it's not a big deal to think about opening the doors in the summer or leaving the shade down.

DONALDSON
What you're addressing is this Industrial Revolution notion of "automatic." That machines will automatically take care of certain functions. In Southern California we have the climatic luxury of questioning things like this. We've been comfortable with designing homes, where you do actively engage with the house as you live in it. You're tuning the architecture. You're paying attention to the weather and your surroundings. You know where you are on the planet and start to engage with nature. We know this is not for everybody!

JOHN WARFEL
Even though we live in an urban setting it is amazing how much more plugged in we are to the fluctuations in the environment because of the design of the house.

SHUBIN
There is an interesting difference between a house that functions like a system versus a living organism. For you, technology has been a tool but you are still in control of the house. It takes your brain to plan how it operates. It's like knowing the tides in the ocean. You're looking ahead, anticipating what tomorrow will be like and planning accordingly.

DEBBIE WARFEL
This idea of "anticipating" also relates to a number of things that we did with regard to the green aspects of the house and some planning that was factored into the construction process. First of all, when we demolished the original house over 90 percent of the materials were recycled. They all went to Habitat for Humanity.

JOHN WARFEL
In demolishing a whole house, maybe one dumpster went to a landfill. Everything was separated on site, bundled, packed on pallets, and taken to Mexico where they were used to build another house for someone. Even though a demo of this kind was more expensive to do, we received a tax credit for it which more than offset the added expense.

DEBBIE WARFEL
That's something that you see happen on commercial projects, and it was an idea that we decided could work with the design of our home.

SHUBIN
Because John is a real estate developer, and was an active participant in the design, it made some of these strategies easier to achieve. We tried to leverage as much architecture and space that we could out of a smaller carbon footprint by just paying a bit more to make the volumes taller.

DEBBIE WARFEL
And the house feels ample because of it, but we don't have any spaces that we don't use everyday.

JOHN WARFEL
But it's very informal. And it has really affected how the family works. For us there is a closeness with our kids, that I'm not sure we would have if we didn't live in a house that is so open.

SHUBIN
It's informing how you live.

DEBBIE WARFEL
We have a family where privacy is not a big issue, and two things have happened. One, the design of the house came from the way we saw ourselves living in it, and because of the design of the house we live in it a certain way. You really have to interact, and the architecture makes you do that.

ABOVE MASTER BATH. PHOTO COURTESY CIRO COELHO.

SANTA BARBARA ESTATE

96-107

SHUBIN
This is a project where we talk explicitly about monumentality and minimalism.

DONALDSON
The client has a beautiful piece of land overlooking the ocean to the south and the mountains to the north. We felt the house needed to have a reciprocity with the scale and magnitude of the landscape. We wanted to maximize the impact of the site and capture the view toward the ocean. It was almost like creating a cinematic drama, where the camera pans across the landscape to make an establishing shot. Each room in the house is designed to frame the site in a different way, and establish a direct relationship between the site and the massing.

SHUBIN
With all of the complexity of our commercial work, we were interested in exploring more elemental ideas in some of our houses, with strong solid volumes juxtaposed with transparent voids.

DONALDSON
Because of their heritage, the clients had an interest in contemporary Mexican architecture. The client wanted a "contemporary home with a Mexican flavor." They asked us to collaborate with Jorge Adler, an architect from Mexico City. We visited Jorge in Mexico City and I was pleased to see our design sensibilities were in sync as they related to scale and massing. We had very similar tastes and design interests. Jorge and his office were great to work with and he was able to source some great Mexican materials and art for the interiors that he did for the home.

SHUBIN
When you first walk into the house the front door frames the ocean in such a way that it feels like it's been integrated into the architecture. It feels like it's part of the house. In California, the indoor-outdoor relationship is a crucial factor in residential design. Part of it is that we have a climate that can support it; and natural conditions like the mountains and the ocean that people want to be connected to, but it also has bearing on social and cultural issues. The same shift that caused a domestication of the office has also caused homes to take on public functions. They're part gallery or gym, or home office.

DONALDSON
People are concerned with how their houses entertain, with how they present themselves publicly. In the United States, houses like these are meant to be de facto public spaces, particularly for people in the entertainment industry where a lot of business positioning happens at social functions. At some level, this public entertaining priority might even usurp certain issues of livability with the house.

SHUBIN
There is also a counterpoint of extreme privatization within the domestic realm. People want to be able to do everything at home, so you end up having to program media rooms and home theatres, gyms, guest houses, the home office, wine cellars, and so on.

DONALDSON
And all authentic civic interaction has just been absorbed into this private domain. Is that a sustainable cultural model? It raises some interesting questions.

TOP EARLY STUDY SKETCH. ROBIN DONALDSON.
BOTTOM MAYAN RUINS AT UXMAL. STONE DETAIL. YUCATAN PENINSULA, MEXICO. PHOTO COURTESY ROBIN DONALDSON.

GREENTREE RESIDENCE

72-79

DONALDSON

We have done a few renovation projects with historically relevant buildings, and this one, although not officially part of the Case Study Program, was of that era. The original house was designed in 1949 by a Los Angeles architect named Kenneth Lind, and was this long glass box perched on steel columns and beams with one end set into the hillside and a garden underneath. Typically houses are oriented toward the street with a proper front façade, but Lind turned the parti of the building so that it opens onto a large side yard, and has no formal entrance. A very cool parti for a home.

SHUBIN

When we started to think about how to engage with this building it seemed important not only to maintain the orientation to the side yard, but to increase the potential for indoor-outdoor living with the additional program we added to the ground floor. The real challenge was doubling the square footage within the envelope of the existing house without drastically altering the aesthetics or how it sat on the site. We kept the ground floor as transparent as possible with big glass windows and doors. We were committed to keeping the original intent of the design by keeping the lower floor all open with glass under the more solid second story above.

DONALDSON

We organized all of the family gathering areas on the ground floor in a very straightforward way... living, dining, kitchen; and then relegated all of the bedrooms to the upper floor, almost like a bridge structure; and then dropped the glazing from the second floor all the way to the ground.

SHUBIN

This is a nice example of a renovation that is ultimately a very environmental kind of a project; taking an existing home, in this case semi-historical, and bringing it back to life so that it functions effectively for a young family at the beginning of the 21st century.

ABOVE MIES VAN DER ROHE. BARCELONA PAVILION. BARCELONA, SPAIN. PHOTO COURTESY ROBIN DONALDSON.

BENTLEY RESIDENCE

108-119

SHUBIN

The principal organizing concept for this project is the large tree in the courtyard. The clients have lived on this property for over thirty years and they have always coordinated their outdoor living around this tree. So the house is designed around it, and the courtyard typology once again is an appropriate design strategy.

DONALDSON

This house is obviously contemporary in its execution and expression, but it is responding to an ancient typology. Fundamentally, this house is a Mediterranean home. Also, this home and other homes we have designed like the Santa Barbara Estate and Riviera all share an element of Neo-Rationalism. They have rationalist tendencies that eschew the complex torque and layered plans of our L.A.-based peers and mentors.

SHUBIN

Well, they all share a quiet monumental scale, and the importance of axial relationships in their floor plans. Like you say, they are actually quite logical and rational. An obvious European influence in that regard.

DONALDSON

When I was in architectural grad school I spent a year in Europe. Living in the Italian speaking canton of Switzerland. I was exposed to a very serious and rigorous school of Ticinese architects who came to teach at Villa SCI-Arc. This was the mid-eighties, and Aldo Rossi and the Italian Neo-Rationalists were big names then in a lot of the mags. Now Aldo didn't show up at our school, but Luigi Snozzi and Mario Botta did. They were fiercely proud of their land and their architectural heritage that they traced their architectural lineage back to Giuseppe Terragni and Casa Del Fascio in nearby Como. In fact one of Snozzi's acolytes showed up at a school party in his father's Italian Fascist uniform. Turns out, a lot of Mussolini's architects jumped the border into Ticino from northern Italy and their descendants are still practicing today under the influence of their fathers and grandfathers.

Now, for a nice surfer dude type kid like myself from sunny Southern California this was a bit of an eye opener. Bumping heads with these politically-driven architects and their acolytes was quite sobering. They mocked all my heroes: Frank Gehry, Eric Moss, and Morphosis. They had a charming little phrase for my heroes' architecture... "masturbato!" (laughs) These Ticinese architects were not interested in "self-expression" or any of Gehry's doodles, chain link, Formica fish, or any other Jungian nonsense related to architecture. They hammered away on us about distilling all architectural ideas and concepts down to their most basic and essential plan and geometry. These guys had a lot of fun with me (especially since they knew I worked for Thom Mayne), and the crits were brutal... but incisive. They talked about the mason who stacks the bricks, the mason who sips the espresso, the mason who is the only one to give an honest day of labor. They tiraded on in Italian about the "strength" of a stone wall, or the meaning of a window lintel, or the long history of architectural vernacular form and they always ended with the same conclusion... why did any of us students think we were smarter than centuries of architectural evolution?

SHUBIN

Yeah, that's a valid question. And to some degree I think we are sympathetic to that point of view...

DONALDSON

Well, certainly to the degree that we, as architectural Modernists at heart, see and appreciate the long evolution of certain forms and architectural strategies that have stood the test of time. The courtyard typology is a great example. Look at the Case Study homes. In Southern California in the '50s and '60s you had Neutra, Ellwood, Koenig, and even Killingsworth, in fact almost all the homes were modern courtyard homes. Hell, look at the Barcelona Pavilion!

SHUBIN

I also think that the courtyard is a very appropriate typology to be working with in the urban realm. You have these urban villas on busy city streets and the façades have very few windows. It's a bit of a defensive stature, but that's the way courtyard homes have been done since the Ottomans. The abstractness of the façade doesn't let on to what's going on inside. There is a hard outer shell that I find aesthetically appealing and appropriate to that site.

DONALDSON

And hopefully our residential work achieves a certain degree of timelessness. We hope that our projects will hold up for a while, in terms of their material integrity and their formal expression. No one will drive by and say... "oh that home is so nineties" or whatever.

SHUBIN

The clients also have an extensive art collection, and we are able to achieve ideal conditions for gallery spaces within the house by locating them all along the east side of the site where the street is. Because of this long monolithic façade we were able to push the house close to the street, gain enough real estate for the galleries, and to open up the other side of the house to the view.

DONALDSON

That openness on the view side of the house is also the result of spaces opening onto the courtyard. Even though this is a fairly large house, it feels intimate because of how the public areas are oriented around that space.

SHUBIN
That was an idea that we really developed when we worked on the homes in Dubai. This project was the next step in a progression of the language from the Santa Barbara Estate, and was pivotal in the Dubai projects.

ABOVE BERBER VILLAGE, ATLAS MOUNTAINS, MOROCCO. PHOTO COURTESY ROBIN DONALDSON.

DAVIDANDGOLIATH

ADVERTISING AGENCY / 120-125

SHUBIN
The client wanted the space to evoke a timeless, worn quality like an old leather book. He believes in the solvency of human artifacts. And even though this was a new ad agency, he wanted to create the impression of permanence. He believes that the company is made up of the history and memories of the people that work there, and he wanted to provide a platform for objects to provoke those memories.

DONALDSON
There were ideas that he had us delve into that were new to us – like the notion of something feeling like it had been there for a long time. We hadn't heard that before, especially from our clients for creative interiors.

SHUBIN
We want the entry to have a primeval feeling, with patinated steel cladding the walls of the lobby. It feels pre-historic, almost like a cave, with the animal-skin rug and David's gigantic slingshot. The reception desk is a monolithic piece of cast stone.

DONALDSON
And then you enter into open spaces that are casual and improvisational.

SHUBIN
But there are still traces of the archetypal materials that you encountered in the lobby and the conference room.The work stations made from basic unfinished materials like wheat board, steel, Homasote, and glass.

DONALDSON
The client had strong feelings about how creative thinking happens; that it doesn't always happen in an office or at a desk. He wanted places to spar ideas. The kitchen and bar, the informal gathering spaces and ping pong tables, as well as the circulation were all organized to instigate free association and cross-pollination among the staff. He wanted to be able to harvest the chance encounters, hot housing, and "eureka in the bathtub" moments which typically arise out of conversations over a meal or two parties brushing past one another on the stairs.

SHUBIN
These spaces were a pathway for unconsciously causing people to experiment and riff. These areas of play were landscapes for creative collaboration and the spontaneous generation of ideas.

DONALDSON
Even though the owner placed a lot on emphasis on the significance of history and temporality, he also wanted the space to have a sense of humor and levity.

SHUBIN
The conceptual basis for the pairing of images on the office doors was rooted in a collective understanding of pop culture. Each sliding office door is screen printed with half of an image. The client wanted to encourage open offices. Typically we think of something being complete when it is closed or continuous, here completion occurs through fragmentation and counter intuition. The printed images on the doors are only complete when two adjacent doors are pushed together and the thresholds into the offices remain open.

ABOVE STEEL DETAIL IN LOBBY. PHOTO COURTESY TOM BONNER.

OGILVY & MATHER

ADVERTISING AGENCY / 126-133

DONALDSON

I've always been really taken with the aerospace industry, the scale and scope of what they do, and the invention and directness of the objects. When we first went to the warehouse that Ground Zero would later occupy, I was very impressed by the 747 fuselage installed in that space. They had filmed Air Force One there and a section of the plane was parked in the middle of the warehouse. That image became lodged in my memory and when we started working on the design for Ogilvy it reemerged. So we built a model of the space and started picking things up around us and putting them into the model. Someone had a piece of tubing that we put in and its scale and form set up well in that large space. We liked its sculptural quality, so we developed it.

SHUBIN

You come into the space from the parking lot and bang right into the side of the tube. Because of the scale and perspective of your approach, it can be a bit disorienting. It is not what you would expect when you come into an advertising agency. This was a way of letting the visitor know that something different was happening here. One side of the building is glass, so it also becomes a way of modulating light and views between the parking lot and the work areas. Because the tube is made of perforated metal, its appearance changes throughout the day. It can appear solid or transparent, depending on the ambient light. We also use the tube to show Ogilvy's work on flat screen monitors. Even though the tube is sculptural, it was also thought of as a processional device that would convey a sense of arrival and transference.

DONALDSON

When we made our initial presentation to the client, we also showed them a couple more conservative design options that didn't have it, but they went for the tube. It's important to understand that they went for the more aggressive option, and that gutsier design choice illustrates their commitment to shift the image of their company via built space.

SHUBIN

They were intent on altering their image, which is why they hired us; a smaller firm willing to experiment. They knew that hiring a big corporate entity like themselves to do the design was most likely not going to get them where they wanted to go. One of the challenges for Ogilvy was to change their corporate culture, but to keep their core values intact. In their previous space the principals of the company were located in corner offices. So we put them in the center of the space to make them more accessible literally and figuratively.

DONALDSON

This is a really large space, and we knew that we needed to respond with design gestures that were proportional in scale. The paneled surfaces are a way of dividing the space into functional areas: reception, work spaces, war rooms, post-production, the library and kitchen. These surfaces function a lot like the scrims in Ground Zero. They are laminated and illustrated with the graphic material that is used to wrap advertising on buses. This is an advertising device, which the client understood. It was their idea to put an image of Ogilvy's face at the end of the tube, as a way to reinforce the history and the attitude of the company.

SHUBIN

Remember, this is not a little idea shop, this is an institution. David Ogilvy is considered the godfather of Madison Avenue advertising and is a legend in the field of advertising and marketing, so these are more than just billboards of the company's branding tactics. This is David Ogilvy, the teacher. He mentored a culture, and these are billboards announcing a value system. They are a call to action!

TOP AIRCRAFT ASSEMBLY PLANT, SOUTHERN CALIFORNIA. GETTY IMAGES.
BOTTOM DETAIL OF THE HOLLYWOOD SIGN FROM BEHIND. GETTY IMAGES.

FUEL DESIGN & PRODUCTION

MOTION GRAPHICS / 140-149
INTERVIEW WITH SETH EPSTEIN, CLIENT

SHUBIN
This was our first office design project, and ultimately the beginning of a long-term relationship with a repeat client.

DONALDSON
Which points to the importance of good clients... people who share our conceptual and philosophical approach. Our work is not just about making buildings, it's also about building businesses and building lives. Seth asked us to do something that seemed impossible; to work on a high design space with a small budget, and a ridiculously fast schedule.

SHUBIN
We didn't know how we were going to get there, and we were willing to say so.

DONALDSON
We are less interested in why we can't do something, and much more engaged in why we can do something. We are more apt to see the possibility in a situation. We look for possibilities. I think that has given us leverage and latitude in situations that other people might not be able to work in.

SHUBIN
There are advantages to tight constraints in the design process, because they force you to design something that is strong and direct. You don't have the luxury to mess with it a lot.

DONALDSON
We could not approach this project from a conventional paradigm. People in the entertainment industry have to be up and running very quickly, so we had to hone in on materials and methods that could fit the ideas, attitude, and budget. We went to places like Home Depot to investigate off-the-shelf materials for lighting, flooring, and structure. It wasn't that we were determined to use gang-nail trusses, per se, but they became a way of making a structure very quickly. We called truss manufacturers that work on tract homes to see how fast they could deliver pieces to the site, once they had drawings. They could do it in a week.

SHUBIN
Even though the methods of construction were fast and things were quick and raw, they were still well crafted. It was really important to us to follow through on the details. When we got there, the existing building shell was in a state of disarray; it was rough and unfinished. Our strategy was to use the rawness of the existing building as a part of our design approach.

DONALDSON
In retrospect that was the most environmentally responsible thing to do; to accept the state of the building, like a found object, and insert architectural elements into the existing shell of the building.

EPSTEIN
At the time, Fuel was a young company, and the state of the building fit the scrappiness of our attitude. We wanted a work-oriented space, with humble materials used very wisely. Our involvement in television informed many of the material choices. There's a luminosity to television. It's backlit. So it made sense that the whole space was lit from behind with transparent panels, and when cars drove by at night and hit their brakes the space would light up like a television screen. One of my favorite things about the space was the conceptual romance and sense of discovery. The 'information bar' was a metaphor that guided people easily through a very big space. It was a bold stroke that dealt with data and information traveling widely over television and the internet, and it set up the context for the work we produced.

SHUBIN
We wanted to express how Fuel functioned through the architecture. We wanted the design to emerge out of their work ethic and attitude.

EPSTEIN
The budget demanded an immense imagination because it was so small, but we were allowed a certain playfulness because we weren't a law firm having depositions and shit. We wanted to have an industrial space with areas of expression that were sensitive to the proclivities of creative people.

DONALDSON
We were fascinated with what Seth's company was doing.

SHUBIN
Their work had a lot of layering, and Seth was intrigued by the ideas of transparency and utility.

DONALDSON
They were using Macintosh computers very early on to do animations. We had the same computers in our office, so we thought we might approach the design by using the same tools. We used the computer to generate a visual tone, and then tone to derive form. It helped communicate a conceptual attitude.

SHUBIN
... and the experience of what it would be like to be in the space. We called our process 'conceptual visualization'. We weren't giving the client renderings of what the space was going to look like, but a visual idea of the approach.

DONALDSON
We built a stage set in the computer to get a feeling for moving through the space. I took video out my car window driving down the freeway, and we fed it into the computer. We moved through it and layered it. We wanted to see how the architecture could employ the resourcefulness of tract home construction in Southern California, the scale of freeway infrastructure, and the ad hoc quality of sound stages and film sets. These influences were not only formal, but they suggested a whole other way of approaching the pace of architecture. We have had clients in the entertainment industry who wonder why it takes so long to build an office when Hollywood can build a film set of an office virtually overnight. In some ways the film industry is a huge bureaucratic industry, just as architecture can be, but it has institutionalized certain ways of working and creating things that are fast and efficient. And we thought maybe there was something to learn from that.

EPSTEIN
You know, architecture has really taught me what I call the "field of dreams" lesson. That space created a future for us that didn't exist at the time. When we first moved in we had an 8,000 square foot space for ten people, and some of them had anxiety that we would never grow to fit that. What's cool about architecture is that it can cause something to happen, because it's physical and real. When you walked into Fuel, you got who we were and where we were going. That space created a demand for something to happen. Architecture can create demand.

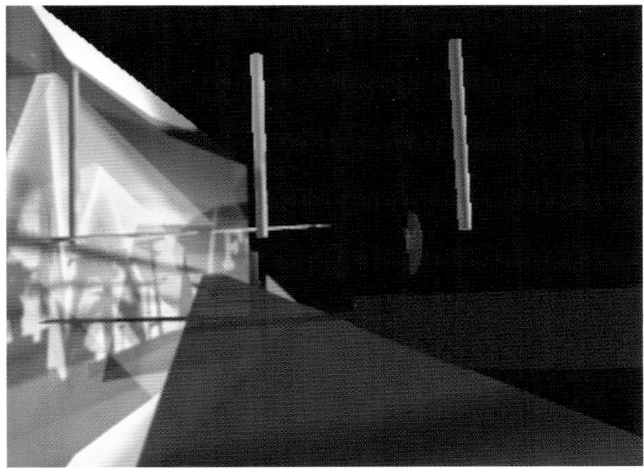

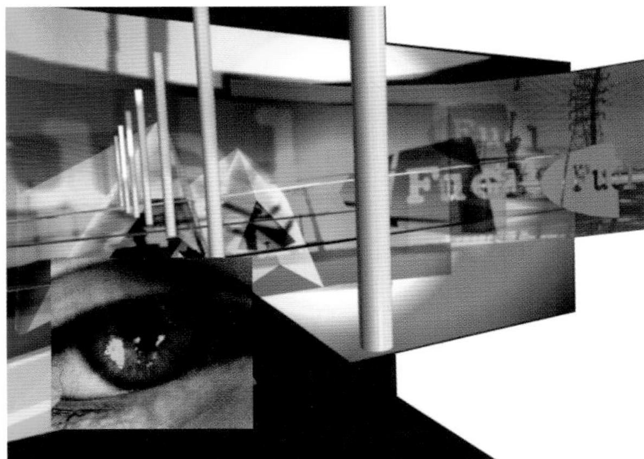

ABOVE FILM AND VIDEO STILLS FOR FUEL. IMAGES COURTESY SHUBIN + DONALDSON ARCHITECTS.

ARTIST STUDIO / GLASS PAVILION

150-157 / 32-37
INTERVIEW WITH ANN DIENER, CLIENT

DONALDSON
We were taking the next design step with the gang-nail trusses like we used on Fuel and wanted to actually make a whole building out of them. An art studio seemed like the perfect project for it. This is a suburban painting studio in a magnificent location, right on an oceanfront bluff between the Santa Ynez Mountains and the Pacific Ocean.

SHUBIN
The positioning of that building is so particular – how it relates to the existing house, the views, the light, the tree that's right next to it. It wasn't open-ended; there was a lot of context to consider. Ann was open to using a language for the studio that differed from the house, but the two still had to relate in some way. We wanted to create a subtle tension between light industrial references and the refined details of a custom residence. The materials ended up being the common language, and they relate in a kind of dance.

DONALDSON
When you first drive in all you can see is the main house and a long shingled wall. At that point the ocean is not even visible. It's not until you come around the corner that the studio announces itself, and the ocean opens up in front of you. We were interested in what you see, what you perceive, the experience being in the building. It's an edited, controlled, scripted experience. It's not an accident.

SHUBIN
We covered the exterior wall with Thermoclear, which we used extensively at Fuel and in other commercial projects, to form a translucent skin that radiates daylight into the spaces. When the lights are on at night, it glows.

DONALDSON
Then we worked on an addition to the main house. The original house, even though it was on the ocean, wasn't really connected to this spectacular location; which was odd, given Ann's relationship to landscape with her work. So we created a glass pavilion to establish a direct connection with site. We imagined them getting up every morning, and having a cup of coffee while the sun rises over the Pacific Ocean.

SHUBIN
Sitting at a Paul Tuttle table.

DONALDSON
Paul designed the table prior to the space being done.

DIENER
Yes, Paul designed the table a few months prior to his passing. I gave him the plans for the room and he worked on the table design for a short period of time each day. Unfortunately, he never saw the finished piece.

DONALDSON
We did the wall with the circle in it as a little homage to Paul. I don't think I would have done that circle without having Paul somehow in my consciousness. And Ann worked on the color for it.

SHUBIN
As an artist, is there a connection between your work and the space of the studio?

DIENER
The scale shift has been significant. I never had a big studio before. The space has a lot to do with the fact that I'm working so large. The new studio is a big enough space that I can do almost anything. So the space really has made a difference in how I work. The light is really good. And it's private space so I can go up there and work without being disturbed.

SHUBIN
Did the content of your work change when the scale of your work shifted?

DIENER
No, but the quality of the work has changed. For some time, I have been working on the changing agricultural landscape of California. Because of the huge studio space, I am able to have all of my sources (books, photographs, and notes) handy and close. I think that this has made the work richer, denser, and more complicated.

DONALDSON
Obviously, as architects, we're having an impact on the environment as well. However, we take the position that man and building and the natural environment can co-exist to the mutual benefit of all.

DIENER
I agree.

DONALDSON
I'm always looking at landscape and in my mind, translating it into architectural form. The terrain we're most connected to is Southern California, particularly Santa Barbara and Los Angeles. We're deliberately regional. We consciously decided to practice on the West Coast. Ann, one of the things that

I've always found really interesting about your work is that it has a regional sensibility and a connection to the history of a place.

SHUBIN
This studio has some of the attitude you see in our commercial work. There isn't the notion of the solid edifice. You see the structure, the skin. It's plastic, in the true sense of the word. It's kind of raw like a mini-warehouse. While we were working on the studio, we were involved in projects like Ground Zero, with the trusses and the prefabrication. We were exploring all those issues. The studio does not have a packaged feeling. It seems like an experiment.

DIENER
Exactly, we didn't know what we were getting when we signed on for this project. We of course saw the plans, but for me, it was hard to translate the drawings into a three-dimensional reality.

DONALDSON
You didn't seem to have any real preconception of what the studio would be.

DIENER
No, just an overall idea. My husband Bob and I have always thought it better to let the architect go ahead and design the space within the general guidelines of the project. We felt that if we interfered too much we would dilute the quality of the architect's work. The spaces that you have designed for us have greatly enhanced the quality of our lives here.

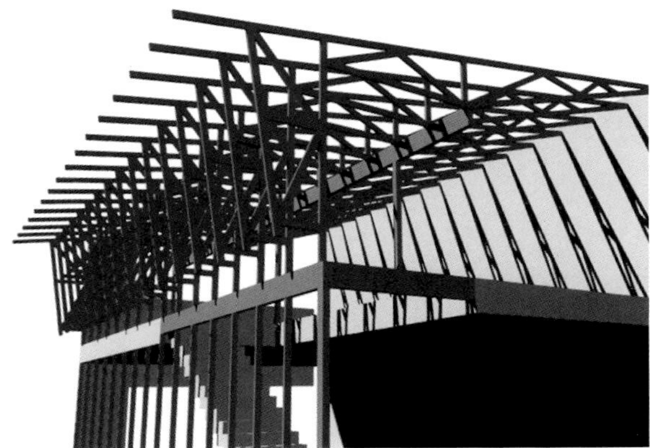

TOP ARTIST STUDIO EARLY STUDY RENDERING. IMAGE COURTESY SHUBIN + DONALDSON ARCHITECTS.
MIDDLE SHUBIN + DONALDSON'S EXHIBITION DESIGN FOR THE PAUL TUTTLE DESIGNS SHOW. UCSB ART MUSEUM. 2001. PHOTO COURTESY WAYNE MCCALL.
BOTTOM ANN DIENER. ENSHROUDED LAND, DETAIL. 2006. IMAGE COURTESY ANN DIENER.

SAATCHI & SAATCHI

ADVERTISING AGENCY / 158-165

DONALDSON

There was a sea change in the mid to late '90s regarding the office environment and accepted norms about how and where the Creative Class works. This project put us in the middle of a company's cultural transformation, and the resultant office retooling. We asked, what's the office of the future for creative companies like advertising agencies? We observed that notebook computers and mobile phones mean work patterns are different. People are no longer bound to their desks and office. Work in a creative company necessitates more elastic and less linear conditions in which to work.

SHUBIN

We're responding to a cultural mandate for new degrees of informality and domestic design qualities in the workplace. Businesses like Saatchi & Saatchi recognize that a lot of professional transaction occurs, and has always occurred, in peripheral social situations; a business meeting at the bar over a scotch and cigar, a few quick words in the elevator and lobby, a lunch meeting at a local café, or in the airport while waiting for a flight. We're interested in the zones where private and professional life overlap.

DONALDSON

Sometimes we wonder why everybody doesn't just work at home? Working at home seems the ultimate conclusion of this shift in work life.

SHUBIN

But that will not happen. People may romanticize the comfort and convenience of working at home, but face-to-face interaction and the creative group mind will not go away. That's why we say if you are not working at home, why not "homing at work"?

DONALDSON

We asked, what constitutes a creative space? Can it be found in something like a kitchen, a living room, a bar, a bathroom? And we proposed that spaces associated with the domestic have creative potential; that an office work station or a conference room are not necessarily where you do your most creative or productive work. The conditions of a home include a wide range of accommodations for living and states of being. However, there is rarely a reciprocal range in the workplace.

SHUBIN

We wondered, what if we could bring to the workplace all the good things that work about a home office? We ended up working with Vitra, who have developed a furniture system called Level 34. Attitudinally, their design borrowed aspects of the home-office environment, like scale and finish, and translated them into commercial furnishings.

DONALDSON

Our strategy, in general, is to generate sensibilities through scale shifts, materials, and furniture with domestic associations that would allow for different creative and socially interactive environments.

SHUBIN

You know, another important factor in shaping the design was that Saatchi had a major internal communication issue. They were spread out evenly over five floors and didn't have spaces that were conducive to collaboration. They also had a very limited budget for this project. So rather than evenly distributing the budget over all five floors, which would only have restated their original situation we chose to densify the individual work station areas. This densification created a series of collective spaces on the third floor (the metaphorical heart of the office), that would act as a destination area, and draw people from their individual work areas to more collaborative spaces.

DONALDSON

It's almost like a land planning scheme or an urban design strategy, where you densify the land use in order to create a larger open space like Central Park. There you can meet in numbers or work in ways that you wouldn't be able to do at your desk. It's where you go for the Revolution!

ABOVE MAYAN RUINS OF UXMAL. NUNNERY COMPLEX. YUCATAN PENINSULA, MEXICO. PHOTO COURTESY ROBIN DONALDSON.

BISCUIT FILMWORKS

FILM PRODUCTION / 166-171

SHUBIN
This project, as well as Brand New School, are a different strain of creative commercial space than much of what we have done in the past. In both cases we discussed notions of "designing background" – making environments that were not distracting and that were conducive to being creative and productive.

DONALDSON
Although we didn't know it when we began this project, this has started to become an emerging philosophy about how we design for creative companies in the recent economic challenging times.

SHUBIN
In the case of Biscuit, the client who is a commercial and film director, was interested in spaces like the Chelsea NY galleries where old warehouses were adapted and reused without compromising the look and feel of the old warehouses. The client was looking for a space that wasn't branded or stylized but maintained the authenticity of the warehouse. They wanted a factory for producing things; a place for making, but the particular of what was being made didn't have to announce itself.

DONALDSON
In many ways this project was a response to the slick, branded contemporary commercial spaces that we see so much of, particularly in Los Angeles. We were all, the client and ourselves, looking to design a space that was more modest, adaptable, and comfortable.

SHUBIN
The fact that we started with found objects, these two old warehouses buildings, was instrumental in developing that sensibility.

DONALDSON
From an environmental "green" standpoint, the adaptive reuse of old buildings has become a really valid branch of work that we do, and I don't think this kind of work will go away. In fact, with the economy and the environment such as they are, we will probably be approached to do more of it.

SHUBIN
So the broad stroke for reusing these buildings is this idea of taking two different warehouses, gutting them, tying them together, and then creating a whole structure inside this grafted building.

DONALDSON
The relationship between the new construction and the old buildings has a subtlety to it that is a bit more complex or nuanced than some of the other commercial spaces we have done. The new components are not always immediately evident.

SHUBIN
We tried to make the new old, or at least that they were not easily distinguishable.

DONALDSON
When you're in the space it's not always easy to tell whether something is part of the original building or whether it's a new piece.

SHUBIN
Like the new curtain wall system. We matched the detailing, sensibility, and scale of the new system to the original shell and the original retrofitting. And we also used the proportions of that system to inform some of the interior wall systems like the conference room and the private offices. That was partially because we did both the shell and core, and the tenant improvement portions of this project. Often you're hired to do one or the other and a lot of time they end up being divorced from each other.

DONALDSON
That sense of blending also comes from the materiality of the project. Using reclaimed wood, handmade tile, ribbed glass, and board-formed concrete, we achieved not only a range of textures and sources, but a kind of industrious spirit that speaks the company's philosophical leanings as a factory for making.

ABOVE MARY BOONE'S CHELSEA GALLERY. NEW YORK, NY. PHOTO COURTESY ADAM SILVERMAN.

TORO CANYON RESIDENCE

172-183
INTERVIEW WITH JOHN MIKE & MARCIA COHEN, CLIENTS

DONALDSON
Every home is a story. And ultimately, a building's meaning is embedded in the materials and form of the structure. The Toro Canyon Residence is a unique tale in many different ways, including how we ended up working together and how you ended up on this site.

JOHN MIKE COHEN
We had wanted to build a house from scratch and we were going to build in Telluride. We had a great site. The house we designed was contemporary, and would not have been visible from any roads, but we had a neighbor who effectively rallied against us.

MARCIA COHEN
He actually told us that we could build the house if we built it with a committee, but he also said, "You need to build in California. This kind of architecture doesn't work here." And lo and behold, we thought maybe that's not a bad idea.

JOHN MIKE COHEN
It was a good idea to build something on the West Coast, because both of our kids are out here. So we started in Vancouver and we drove down the coast on Highway 1 looking for a place to build.

MARCIA COHEN
Santa Barbara was our last stop on that trip and so far [we had] no luck on any viable sites. So when we made it to Santa Barbara, and looked at this property in Toro Canyon we ended up making a ridiculous and impulsive decision. We actually bought the property on that trip. Just like that.

JOHN MIKE COHEN
Then I spent a year working on and refining a design, which is what I brought to you when we first met. We wanted to interview local architects and contractors at the same time and we were recommended to you because of your jurisdictional savvy. And lo and behold, what we found was a design sensitivity that we could relate to in terms of detailing and moving the project forward. Of the people that we interviewed there was no question that I was more sympathetic with your work than anyone else's.

DONALDSON
There were two aspects that made it an interesting prospect for us. One was that I liked the design and where you were coming from, and knew that there weren't too many people in Santa Barbara that could work on this project with you guys and pull it off. Knowing the jurisdictional issues and the fact that I liked where you were coming from started to add up to a situation that I thought could be productive and interesting for the office. We've had a history of working with other architects on projects in different capacities; where we've been the design architect and they have been the executive architect, and vice versa. I have found each time that we've done that, that we've learned something and usually it's been a good professional experience. You look at the project in terms of the office, and determine whether this is something that the staff is going to want to be a part of; will it settle in and fit within our value system? The building design fits tightly within our approach to practicing architecture, particularly the materiality, the attitude, and how it relates to its challenging but beautiful site.

MARCIA COHEN
There were some conditions of the site that were potentialities, and not simply challenges. Very early on it was suggested that we could harvest and mill some of the eucalyptus trees on the property, and use that lumber for the wood in the house. In the end it was a very complicated process and I'm not sure it is something that we would do again, but conceptually and philosophically, it is nice to know that much of the wood in the house came from a stand of trees just outside, and that there is a literal material connection between the house and the site.

JOHN MIKE COHEN
I really wanted the living space to be one large volume with a lot of glazing on both sides, so that when you were in it, you really felt the presence of the environment around you. That's how the two living volumes got separated and the linking piece became glass. The idea was to negate the link. The entry hall was always thought of as an outdoor space. We talked about this conceptually, and the idea is that you actually enter the house when you turn the corner and go into that living volume; not when you walk into to the glass piece, that's just the preamble. Interestingly, the house has turned out to be very castle-like. I think it has something to do with the concrete and the height of the volumes. You can imagine a fire in the fireplace.

MARCIA COHEN
I suppose there is a historic architectural interpretation in there, but we're talking sixteenth century; the translation of which is thoroughly contemporary. And the image that you carried about this house evolved, as the design underwent a series of relocations and reincarnations over the past six years.

DONALDSON

Even though there was a lot of massaging the design, the basic parti remained solid throughout the project. There is a monumental quality to the house, which is also present in many of the residential projects that we have designed. This is probably part of the reason that we were sympathetic to one another; but I don't think that the design is out of proportion for the site. The dramatic site demands a scale and bold stroke. No mumbling in that big dramatic canyon; it calls for spaces that respond in kind.

ABOVE MODELS STUDYING RELATIONSHIP OF MASSING TO SITE. PHOTOS COURTESY SHUBIN + DONALDSON ARCHITECTS.

THE FIRM
TALENT AGENCY / 184-189

DONALDSON
Looking at this project, one would never guess that it sits on the ground floor of a 20-story building on Wilshire Boulevard. Or that it was a conversion of a marble clad bank branch from the 1960s.

SHUBIN
Only in Beverly Hills would you get to convert an old bank into offices for a hip young talent agency like The Firm.

DONALDSON
The existing high rise building is a fairly typical '60s Wilshire Boulevard office building. The exterior of the old bank space is surrounded with dark tinted glass and getting some natural light into the space was a real challenge. After stripping the old marble we discovered a good, basic, reinforced concrete shell.

SHUBIN
And this space has a 30-foot ceiling, which is a very high ceiling for an office high-rise building. There were spatial challenges, in terms of infrastructure and lighting, and we couldn't touch the existing building, so we created a structure within the structure.

DONALDSON
The partners wanted their offices on the perimeter of the space by the windows and the assistants sit in bullpens on the inside of the space. We wanted to get natural light... or at least the illusion of natural light into the center of the space. Therefore we created a backlit glass façade that wrapped around an interior courtyard we formed with the perimeter office structure. This internal frosted glass façade defined a private office corridor and filled the space with light. It also concealed all of the ductwork and mechanical units. This interior glass façade also has the feel of being on the exterior of the building, and with the exterior light coming through it really makes the space glow.

SHUBIN
With the partners in perimeter offices and the assistants in the middle of this two-story space, it reminds me of the main floor in Frank Lloyd Wright's Johnson Wax building. Tall columns grounded by workstations and light working its way into the space.

SHUBIN
The client also needed a gathering space that could accommodate everyone in the company. We designed a bleacher system in the conference room which wraps up the wall and ceiling and transitioned into a sound baffling wall and ceiling assembly. We wanted the furniture and the space to be one continuous piece, and it alluded to ship hulls and stadiums. We also wanted to retain the urban memory of the bank, so we converted the vault into a lounge.

ABOVE ORIGINAL BANK VAULT CONVERTED INTO LOUNGE. PHOTO COURTESY TOM BONNER.

HYDRAULX

SPECIAL EFFECTS / 134-139

SHUBIN

Hydraulx is a special-effects house for big feature films. It's run by the Strause brothers, who are very aggressive in how they go about their work. They wear army fatigues everyday. They're in the trenches, and there is a lot of vigor to their work. They have two 12 hour shifts, so their studios are running 24 hours a day, seven days a week.

DONALDSON

They attack their work like a military defense contractor, which is probably what they have to do to compete. The schedules for these feature films and television shows are demanding, and because they're engaged in a creative process, there's no guarantee how long things are going to take. They have to create the illusion of things blowing up, ships sinking, buildings falling over, tsunamis wiping out entire cities. They collect and study a broad range of objects and images and use them to create some incredible cutting-edge visualization.

SHUBIN

The brothers are fascinated by the grit and substance of objects and materials. People that work with simulations and ephemera need tactile and corporeal experience. So we wanted to give them an architecture that was honest and direct in its material execution. We used a number of basic materials like steel, wood, and glass, and carefully tracked their articulation and detailing.

DONALDSON

And the space planning is rather intricate. Some spaces are very compact and others are expansive.

SHUBIN

The machine room is a focal point above the entry, and can be seen from almost anywhere within the space. This room powers all of the sophisticated technology that they use to generate their work, so we wanted the architecture to express the importance of these operations. We turned cable management into a design opportunity, and articulated the overhead steel cages threading throughout the space. The visible route of computer cables is integrated into the architectural details.

ABOVE MACHINE ROOM. PHOTO COURTESY TOM BONNER.

PAINTER RESIDENCE

190-195
INTERVIEW WITH SCOTT PAINTER, CLIENT

PAINTER
The history of the property is pretty interesting. It's located on a natural bluff in Moraga Canyon, Bel Air. It was originally owned by a guy named Bill Berry. He was recruited by Howard Hughes to come out to California and be the chief engineer for the Spruce Goose. As part of his signing bonus, he was given 1,000 acres in Bel Air that stretched from Sepulveda all the way up to Mulholland Drive, so at one point all of Moraga Canyon was owned by Bill. He lived there for 46 years, and raised ten children there.

When Bill worked for Hughes Aircraft he traveled all over the world, and because he didn't have to go through customs he would bring back saplings of things like Chinese Elms. So now the canyon and our property are full of rare and extinct trees, and in the fall you can witness the "Connecticut Effect," where all of the trees change color, which is something that you don't normally see with the vegetation that's native to Los Angeles.

When Bill retired he made his living by selling off parcels of his land. He gave 536 acres to the Santa Monica Mountain Conservancy, so everything to our north is unbuilt native land. He sold a large portion to Tom Jones who once ran Northrop Grummond, and is responsible for the B1 bomber. And Tom used that land to develop Moraga Vineyard, which is the only licensed vineyard in LA.

Now one day I was at the TED conference (technology, entertainment, and design) up in Monterey, which I go to every year. And I met a guy who is sort of a modern-day Ansel Adams. He had bought all of the camera equipment out of the belly of the SR71 spy plane when they retired the program. He creates photos of landscapes with so much resolution that if you looked at a cityscape of New York, you could peer into the windows of every hotel room, and see what's on every desk. It was one of the most fascinating pictures that I had ever seen because you could just look into it forever. So I said to him, "I've got this great view of the Getty. You can come and photograph it from my house." We stalked the weather and waited for a day in March when the Santa Ana's came in and blew out all of the clouds and smog. We had this 4' x 8' photograph printed, which was quite expensive, and I'd had it for a day when I decided that I had to meet Tom Jones, the guy who owns the vineyard in the canyon, because it's so prominent in the foreground of this picture. I called the winery out of the phonebook and a man answered the phone. I said, "I live up the hill and I'd really like to meet you. I've got something for you." So I put the picture in the truck and drove down the hill. I gave him the photograph and he started to cry. I had no idea that at one point he had owned all of the land under the Getty, and when he made the deal with the Getty, he had them create a conservancy so that all of that land could never be built on. He gave us saplings from his vineyard, and I became very interested in creating a vineyard on our property, to reconnect the land with the history of the canyon, and restore the sense of what the land had been.

DONALDSON
This is a real soft spot for us; the stories that places carry and how those stories can inform a design strategy. We're interested in the potential for regenerative forms of land planning and conservation. How do you think you'd be able to fold yourself into the viniculture of the canyon?

PAINTER
Well, our acreage would be a significant expansion to the vineyard, and harvesting is a lot of work. Tom is 84 years old, so he doesn't want to do it himself, but I would find a way to make sure that our grapes made it into the Moraga bottles. You can't buy his wine in stores. You have to buy it directly from Tom. So I've started buying it and giving it to everyone I know, because it's like our own signature neighborhood wine.

DONALDSON
Hopefully these ideas of regionalism, local consumption, and artisanal making will come back into people's consciousness about the impact of how we consume and build. In some ways they need to, and I think the history of the land that you are now contributing to is a great model.

PAINTER
Another significant influence came when I heard Bill McDonough talk about environmental architecture at that same TED conference. I thought it was so smart, because you can get all the imperfections of nature, but build something that you can really live in. One of the things that really impressed me were the buildings with lawn and terrain on the roof. I immediately thought we could do that for our house. Wouldn't it be great to have nature up there, with a yard on the roof? I had no idea how you could make that a reality, but I was just amused that you could do it. The idea I had for this house was a combination of McDonough's influence, and an experience that I had growing up in the Pacific Northwest. We had a neighbor that had a 200-foot rusty tug boat. He could certainly afford a beautiful Hatteras yacht, but instead he tooled around in this jalopy which was the topic of conversation on the island. One day I finally got a tour of the tugboat. The tugboat looked awful from the outside, but what no one knew is that on the inside it was the nicest yacht you'd ever seen. It was so cool and understated. I thought that was sophisticated, the idea of not showing it on the outside.

SHUBIN

This is an idea that we have explored in some of our work. We are interested in the process of divulging. The idea of suppressing or hiding certain elements, and then exposing them as you move through a sequence, as you enter the building.

DONALDSON

We've had an interest in not telling you everything at once, or not divulging everything upfront. Some houses have a particular street presence where they tell you something about status or social standing. Many of our designs slowly reveal themselves or are understated. Our approach to green issues is often addressed this way. They don't announce themselves immediately or through a demonstration of devices or technology, unless it is part of our intention.

PAINTER

I imagine very little perceivable "built" presence. The entrance is marked by this single low wall that cuts into the land and slips down into the house. It is this subtle but somehow dramatic transition from the natural environment to a built, modern one. I really love the over-sized proportions and the permanence of the stone at the Getty Center; how it looks so institutional and permanent. It's not going anywhere. Most houses look so temporary to me, that they're not going to stand the test of time. I think that's captured in the concept; the monumental proportions, with big living spaces, and it would all be underneath the vineyard. Because of the nature of the property on the promontory, you wouldn't feel like you were living in the earth. You would have sweeping views and be able to see through the house. I can't live without a view. I have to see the horizon line in order to get comfortable. That is absolutely what resets me everyday.

DONALDSON

It's interesting that you mention the Getty, because in some ways this is the anti-Getty. When Russell and I were trained as architects we were indoctrinated into the International Style of Le Corbusier, and global modern architecture. The Getty Center is of that pedigree. It exists regardless of its context in many ways. Here we were interested in swinging back to regional and contextual issues that take into account social milieu and land use history.

SHUBIN

This house and the Getty are quite different. This house is like a series of rock outcroppings; it's an architectonic extension of the natural topography that embraces the phenomenon of living within the earth; whereas the Getty is more like a public sculpture sitting on a granite plinth which crowns nature. This house creates an experience that is rooted in the social and natural history of the place and couldn't exist anywhere else.

ABOVE LIGHT WELL IN LE CORBUSIER'S ABBEY OF LA TOURETTE. PHOTO COURTESY HEATHER PETERSON.

INDEX

GROUND ZERO MARINA DEL REY, CA / 1999 **PARTNERS IN CHARGE** ROBIN DONALDSON, AIA / RUSSELL SHUBIN, AIA **PROJECT MANAGER** AUSTIN KELLY **PROJECT TEAM** JOSH BLUMER / RYAN IHLY / MINA JAVID / BRENNAN LINDNER **STRUCTURAL ENGINEER** RAFFI ABKARIAN **MECHANICAL ENGINEER** MB&A **ELECTRICAL ENGINEER** V&M **LIGHTING DESIGN** HORTON-LEES **CONTRACTOR** BECKER GENERAL CONTRACTORS **PHOTOGRAPHER** TOM BONNER / JIMMY COHRSSEN **SIZE** 20,000 SF

006 / 007

008 / 009

016 / 017

MINDFIELD MARINA DEL REY, CA / 2000 **PARTNERS IN CHARGE** ROBIN DONALDSON, AIA / RUSSELL SHUBIN, AIA **PROJECT MANAGER** AUSTIN KELLY **PROJECT TEAM** FRED BESANCON / JOSH BLUMER / JIM DAVIS / MARK GEE / RYAN IHLY / MINA JAVID / BRENNAN LINDNER / SHANE RYMER **CONTRACTOR** SIERRA PACIFIC CONSTRUCTORS **PHOTOGRAPHER** TOM BONNER **SIZE** 20,000 SF

018 / 019

MONTECITO RESIDENCE MONTECITO, CA / 2000 **PARTNERS IN CHARGE** ROBIN DONALDSON, AIA / RUSSELL SHUBIN, AIA **PROJECT MANAGER** RYAN IHLY **PROJECT TEAM** FRED BESANCON / JOSH BLUMER / GORDON BREWER / JIM DAVIS / ANAT GOTTSMAN / BRENNAN LINDNER **LANDSCAPE ARCHITECT** KATHRYN DOLE ASSOCIATES **CONTRACTOR** LOPRESTI CONSTRUCTION **PHOTOGRAPHER** TOM BONNER **SIZE** 3,800 SF

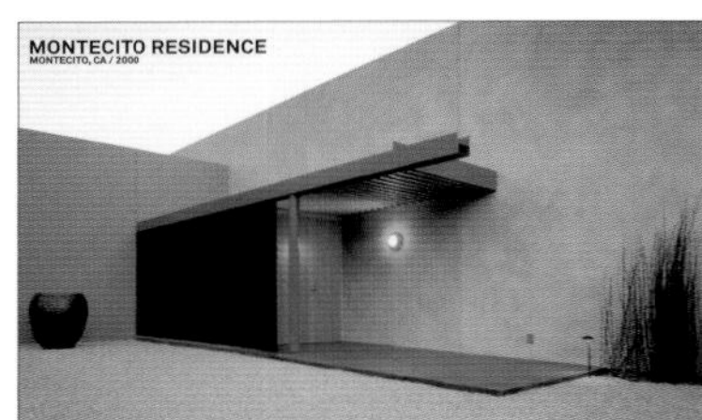

026 / 027

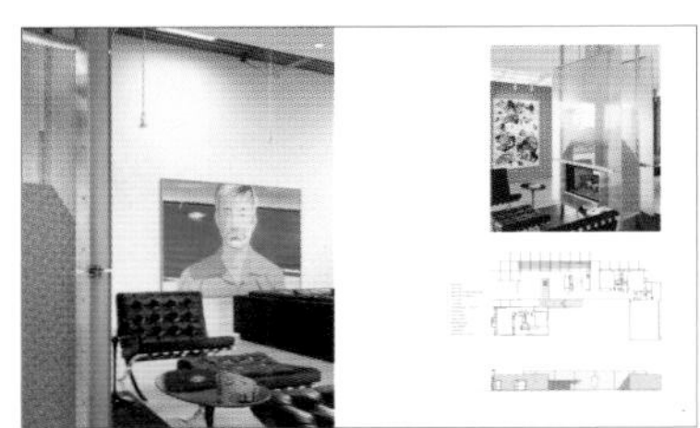

028 / 029

034 / 035

036 / 037

URBAN SPA MALIBU, CA / 2002 **PARTNERS IN CHARGE** ROBIN DONALDSON, AIA / RUSSELL SHUBIN, AIA **PROJECT TEAM** MARK HERSHMAN / MARK GEE / MINA JAVID **INTERIOR DESIGN CONSULTANT** AUDREY ALBERTS **CONTRACTOR** QUILLIN CONSTRUCTION **PHOTOGRAPHER** TOM BONNER **SIZE** 2,900 SF

044 / 045

BRAND NEW SCHOOL SANTA MONICA, CA / 2005 **PARTNERS IN CHARGE** ROBIN DONALDSON, AIA / RUSSELL SHUBIN, AIA **PROJECT MANAGER** MARK HERSHMAN **PROJECT TEAM** EUN SUNG LEE / MICHAEL TADROS **CONTRACTOR** SIERRA PACIFIC CONSTRUCTORS **PHOTOGRAPHER** TOM BONNER **SIZE** 10,500 SF

046 / 047

010 / 011

012 / 013

014 / 015

020 / 021

022 / 023

024 / 025

030 / 031

GLASS PAVILION SANTA BARBARA, CA / 2006 **PARTNERS IN CHARGE** ROBIN DONALDSON, AIA / RUSSELL SHUBIN, AIA **PROJECT MANAGER** JOSH BLUMER **PROJECT TEAM** FRED BESANCON **STRUCTURAL ENGINEER** EDL STRUCTURAL **CONTRACTOR** SCOTT GREGORY **PHOTOGRAPHER** CIRO COELHO **SIZE** 200 SF

032 / 033

038 / 039

040 / 041

042 / 043

048 / 049

050 / 051

WONG DOODY CULVER CITY, CA / 2006 **PARTNERS IN CHARGE** ROBIN DONALDSON, AIA / RUSSELL SHUBIN, AIA **PROJECT MANAGER** MARK HERSHMAN **PROJECT TEAM** DAVID O'BRIAN / MICHAEL TADROS / CHRIS WEBB **STRUCTURAL ENGINEER** JOHN LABIB & ASSOCIATES **MECHANICAL ENGINEER** AIR PRODUCTS **ELECTRICAL ENGINEER** CALIFORNIA INDUSTRIAL **LIGHTING DESIGNER** LIGHTING DESIGN ALLIANCE **CONTRACTOR** SPEER CONSTRUCTION **PHOTOGRAPHER** TOM BONNER **SIZE** 13,500 SF

052 / 053

054 / 055

056 / 057

062 / 063

064 / 065

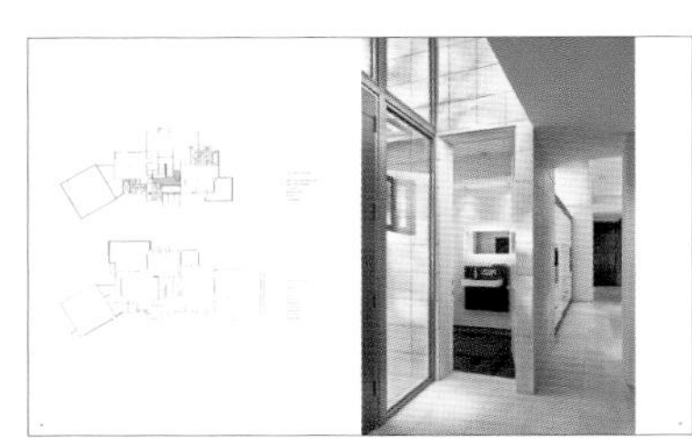

066 / 067

072 / 073

074 / 075

076 / 077

082 / 083

084 / 085

086 / 087

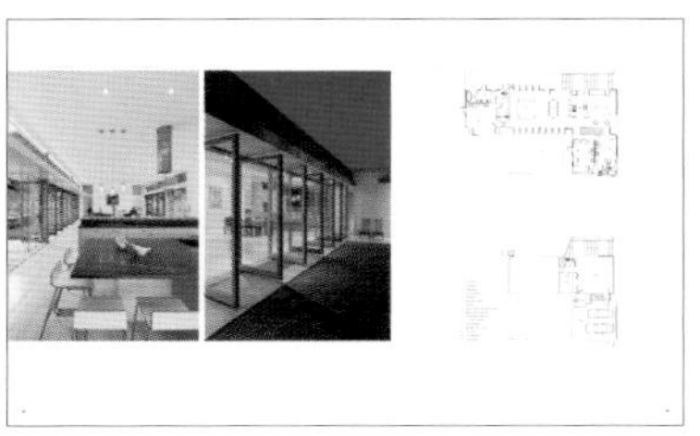

092 / 093

094 / 095

SANTA BARBARA ESTATE SANTA BARBARA, CA / 2003 **PARTNERS IN CHARGE** ROBIN DONALDSON, AIA / RUSSELL SHUBIN, AIA / JORGE ADLER, ADLER ARQUITECTOS, MEXICO CITY **PROJECT MANAGERS** CLAY AURELL / SERAFIN LUZ, ADLER ARQUITECTOS **PROJECT TEAM** FRED BESANCON / JOSH BLUMER **INTERIOR DESIGN** LOURDES APODACA, ADLER ARQUITECTOS **LANDSCAPE ARCHITECT** KATHYRN DOLE ASSOCIATES **CONTRACTOR** CRAWFORD CONSTRUCTION **PHOTOGRAPHER** CIRO COELHO **SIZE** 10,500 SF

058 / 059

RIVIERA RESIDENCE SANTA BARBARA, CA / 2006 **PARTNERS IN CHARGE** ROBIN DONALDSON, AIA / RUSSELL SHUBIN, AIA **PROJECT ARCHITECT** ROBIN DONALDSON, AIA **PROJECT TEAM** JOSH BLUMER / NILS HAMMERBECK / KELLY KISH / ALAN MCLEOD / DAVID VAN HOY / DANIEL WEBBER / ALLISON WHITE **INTERIOR DESIGNER** GENIE GABLE **LANDSCAPE ARCHITECT** LANE GOODKIND **CONTRACTOR** QUILLIN CONSTRUCTION **PHOTOGRAPHER** CIRO COELHO **SIZE** 3,200 SF

060 / 061

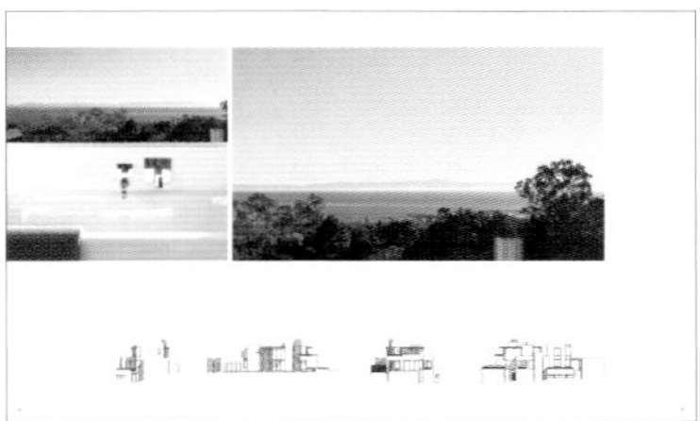

068 / 069

070 / 071

GREENTREE RESIDENCE PACIFIC PALISADES, CA / 2006 **PARTNERS IN CHARGE** ROBIN DONALDSON, AIA / RUSSELL SHUBIN, AIA **PROJECT MANAGER** MARK HERSHMAN **PROJECT TEAM** AMANDA TRUEMPER **CONTRACTOR** MINARDOS CONSTRUCTION **PHOTOGRAPHER** CIRO COELHO **SIZE** 2,350 SF

078 / 079

DUBAI VILLAS DUBAI, UNITED ARAB EMIRATES / 2008 **PARTNERS IN CHARGE** ROBIN DONALDSON, AIA / RUSSELL SHUBIN, AIA **PROJECT ARCHITECTS** GREG GRIFFIN / ALAN MCLEOD **PROJECT TEAM** TIM GORTER / BRAD KELLEY / KEVIN MOORE / LAUREN ANDERSON / HEATHER PETERSON / KEIKO OKADA / ISAAC HENDRICKS / JOSH HARRISON / NEPTALI CISNEROS **RENDERINGS** CRYSTAL DIGITAL TECHNOLOGY **SIZE** 3,937 SF / 6,561 SF / 13,451 SF

080 / 081

088 / 089

EAST CHANNEL RESIDENCE SANTA MONICA, CA / 2006 **PARTNERS IN CHARGE** ROBIN DONALDSON, AIA / RUSSELL SHUBIN, AIA **PROJECT MANAGER** MARK HERSHMAN **PROJECT TEAM** MICHAEL TADROS / DAVID O'BRIAN **CONTRACTOR** LFA CONSTRUCTION **PHOTOGRAPHER** CIRO COELHO **SIZE** 4,400 SF

090 / 091

096 / 097

098 / 099

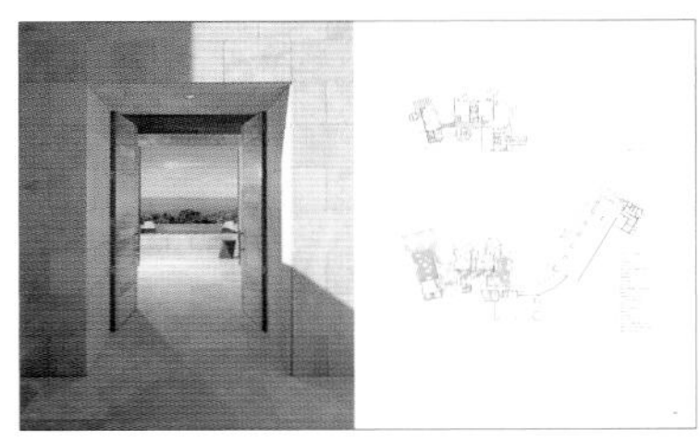

100 / 101

102 / 103

104 / 105

106 / 107

112 / 113

114 / 115

116 / 117

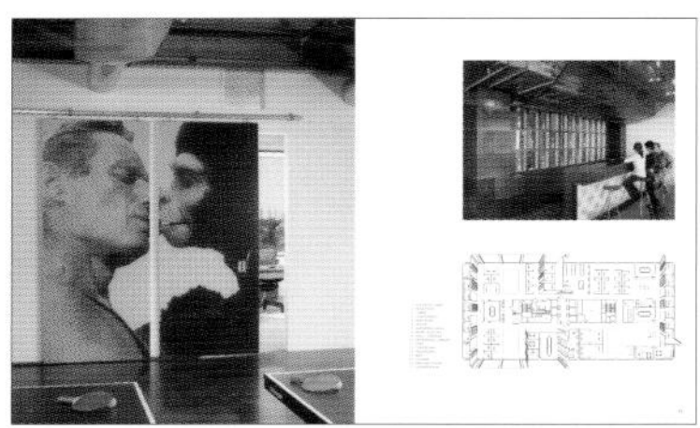

122 / 123

124 / 125

OGILVY & MATHER CULVER CITY, CA / 2000 **PARTNERS IN CHARGE** ROBIN DONALDSON, AIA / RUSSELL SHUBIN, AIA **PROJECT MANAGERS** SEAN HAGAN / JOSH BLUMER **PROJECT TEAM** MAHYAR ABOUSAEEDI / FRED BESANCON / MARK GEE / MARK HERSHMAN / MINA JAVID / BRENNAN LINDNER / ROB SUTMAN **SHELL AND CORE ARCHITECT** ERIC OWEN MOSS **MECHANICAL ENGINEER** FRUCHTMAN & ASSOCIATES **ELECTRICAL ENGINEER** PAUL IMMERMAN **LIGHTING CONSULTANT** LIGHTING DESIGN ALLIANCE **CONTRACTOR** SIERRA PACIFIC CONSTRUCTORS **PHOTOGRAPHER** TOM BONNER **SIZE** 30,000 SF

132 / 133

HYDRAULX SANTA MONICA, CA / 2007 **PARTNERS IN CHARGE** ROBIN DONALDSON, AIA / RUSSELL SHUBIN, AIA **PROJECT ARCHITECT** ANN-SOFI HOLST **PROJECT TEAM** MICHAEL ASHWORTH / AMANDA TRUEMPER / CHRIS WEBB **STRUCTURAL ENGINEER** JOHN LABIB & ASSOCIATES **MECHANICAL / ELECTRICAL ENGINEER** HI-TECH ENGINEERS **CONTRACTOR** SIERRA PACIFIC CONSTRUCTORS **LIGHTING DESIGNER** LIGHTING DESIGN ALLIANCE **ACOUSTICIAN** STUDIO 440 **AV CONSULTANT** VISIONEERING DESIGN COMPANY **PHOTOGRAPHER** TOM BONNER **SIZE** 15,000 SF

134 / 135

140 / 141

142 / 143

144 / 145

BENTLEY RESIDENCE BEL AIR, CA / 2008 **PARTNERS IN CHARGE** ROBIN DONALDSON, AIA / RUSSELL SHUBIN, AIA **PROJECT ARCHITECT** ANN-SOFI HOLST **PROJECT TEAM** CHRIS GARZA / LUIS GOMEZ **CONTRACTOR** PORTER DEVELOPMENT **PHOTOGRAPHER** CIRO COELHO **SIZE** 6,950 SF

108 / 109

110 / 111

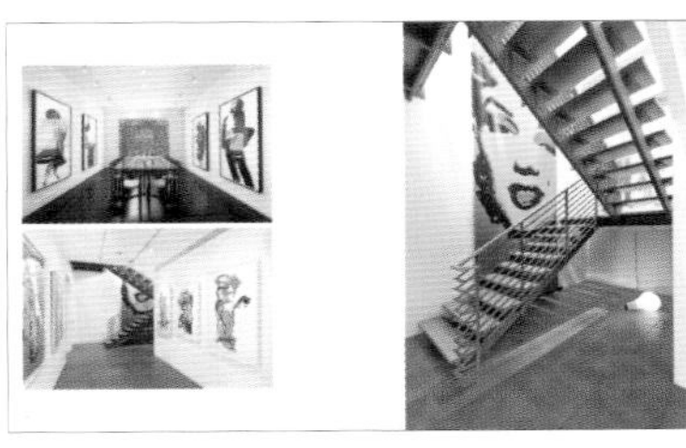

118 / 119

DAVIDANDGOLIATH EL SEGUNDO, CA / 2006 **PARTNER IN CHARGE** RUSSELL SHUBIN, AIA **PROJECT ARCHITECT** ANN-SOFI HOLST **PROJECT TEAM** MARK HERSHMAN / DAVID O'BRIAN / CHRIS WEBB **CONTRACTOR** SIERRA PACIFIC CONSTRUCTORS **LIGHTING DESIGNER** LIGHTING DESIGN ALLIANCE **PHOTOGRAPHER** TOM BONNER **SIZE** 30,300 SF

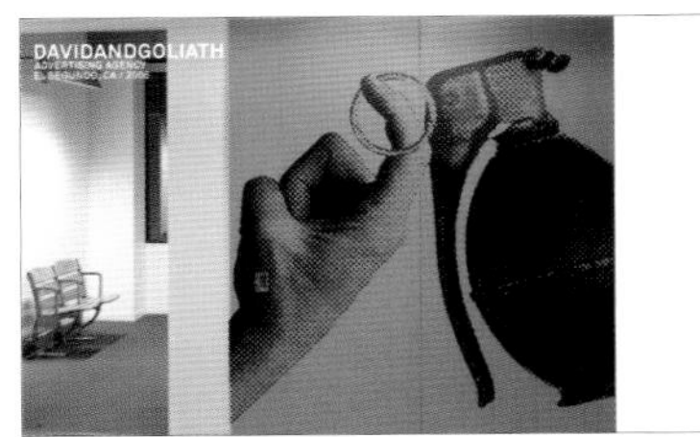

120 / 121

126 / 127

128 / 129

130 / 131

136 / 137

138 / 139

FUEL DESIGN & PRODUCTION SANTA MONICA, CA / 1998 **PARTNERS IN CHARGE** ROBIN DONALDSON, AIA / RUSSELL SHUBIN, AIA **PROJECT MANAGER** RYAN IHLY **PROJECT TEAM** JOSH BLUMER / ANAT GOTTSMAN **CONTRACTOR** LOPRESTI CONSTRUCTION **PHOTOGRAPHER** FARSHID ASSASSI / TOM BONNER **SIZE** 8,000 SF

146 / 147

148 / 149

ARTIST STUDIO SANTA BARBARA, CA / 2002 **PARTNERS IN CHARGE** ROBIN DONALDSON, AIA / RUSSELL SHUBIN, AIA **PROJECT MANAGER** JOSH BLUMER **PROJECT TEAM** FRED BESANCON **STRUCTURAL ENGINEER** EDL STRUCTURAL **CONTRACTOR** SCOTT GREGORY **PHOTOGRAPHER** CIRO COELHO **SIZE** 1,700 SF

150 / 151

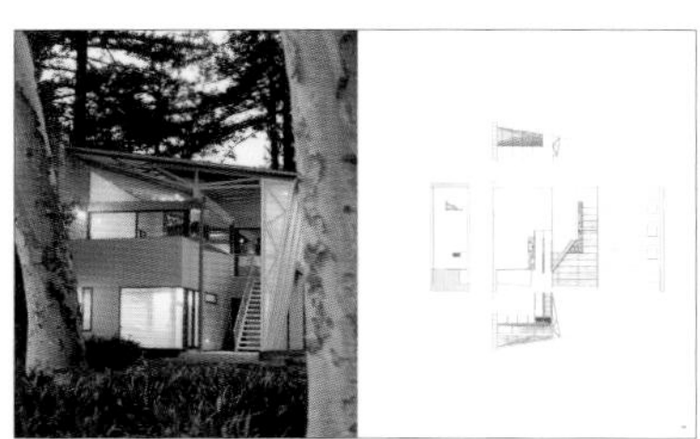

152 / 153

154 / 155

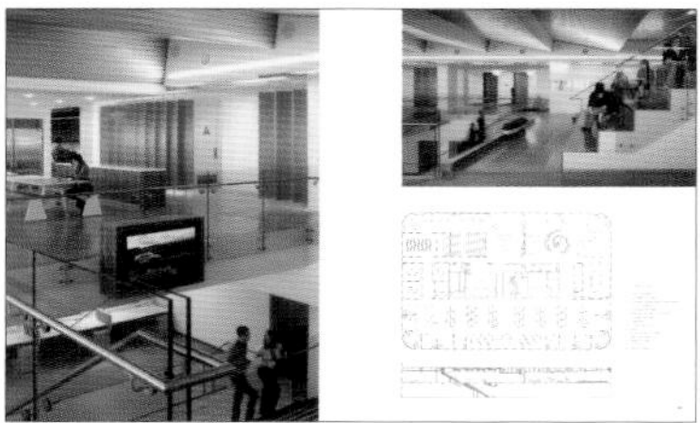

160 / 161

162 / 163

164 / 165

170 / 171

TORO CANYON RESIDENCE SANTA BARBARA, CA / 2009 **PARTNER IN CHARGE** ROBIN DONALDSON, AIA **DESIGN ARCHITECT** JOHN MIKE COHEN **PROJECT ARCHITECT** GREG GRIFFIN **PROJECT TEAM** SHEIDA OWRANG / KARL HAMILTON **MEP ENGINEER** MECHANICAL ENGINEERING CONSULTANTS **STRUCTURAL ENGINEER** TAYLOR & SYFAN CONSULTING **CONTRACTOR** PAUL FRANZ CONSTRUCTION **LANDSCAPE ARCHITECT** LANE GOODKIND **PHOTOGRAPHER** CIRO COELHO

172 / 173

180 / 181

182 / 183

THE FIRM BEVERLY HILLS, CA / 2002 **PARTNERS IN CHARGE** ROBIN DONALDSON, AIA / RUSSELL SHUBIN, AIA **PROJECT MANAGER** MARK HERSHMAN **PROJECT TEAM** MARK GEE / MINA JAVID / ISRAEL KANDARIAN **MEP ENGINEER** SIMON WONG & ASSOCIATES **STRUCTURAL ENGINEER** DTA CONSULTING ENGINEERS **CONTRACTOR** SIERRA PACIFIC CONSTRUCTORS **LIGHTING DESIGN** LIGHTING DESIGN ALLIANCE **METALWORK** HYPEARC **PHOTOGRAPHER** TOM BONNER **SIZE** 8,500 SF

PAINTER RESIDENCE BEL AIR, CA / DESIGNED 2006 **PARTNERS IN CHARGE** ROBIN DONALDSON, AIA / RUSSELL SHUBIN, AIA **PROJECT MANAGER** BRAD KELLEY **SIZE** 26,800 SF

190 / 191

192 / 193

156 / 157

SAATCHI & SAATCHI TORRANCE, CA / 2008 **PARTNERS IN CHARGE** ROBIN DONALDSON, AIA / RUSSELL SHUBIN, AIA **PROJECT MANAGER** MARK HERSHMAN **PROJECT TEAM** LUIS GOMEZ / CHRIS WEBB / BRYAN FLAIG / KEIKO OKADA / REID EMBREY **CONTRACTOR** SIERRA PACIFIC CONSTRUCTORS **PHOTOGRAPHER** TOM BONNER **SIZE** 106,000 SF

158 / 159

BISCUIT FILMWORKS HOLLYWOOD, CA / 2009 **PARTNERS IN CHARGE** ROBIN DONALDSON, AIA / RUSSELL SHUBIN, AIA **PROJECT MANAGER** MARK HERSHMAN **PROJECT TEAM** ERIC SCHONSETT / CHRIS WEBB **MEP ENGINEER** SIMON WONG & ASSOCIATES **STRUCTURAL ENGINEER** GRIMM & CHEN STRUCTURAL **CONTRACTOR** SIERRA PACIFIC CONSTRUCTORS **PHOTOGRAPHER** TOM BONNER **SIZE** 10,800 SF

166 / 167

168 / 169

174 / 175

176 / 177

178 / 179

184 / 185

186 / 187

188 / 189

194 / 195

BIOGRAPHIES

RUSSELL SHUBIN AIA, LEED AP, was born in Los Angeles, CA in 1960, and studied architecture at California Polytechnic University at San Luis Obispo, where he received his Bachelor of Architecture degree in 1985. He also studied at L'Ecole d'Art et d'Architecture at Fountainebleau, France, during 1984. Russell began practicing in 1985 with the Blurock Partnership in Newport Beach, CA, a nationally recognized firm that has received numerous AIA awards. Shortly after becoming an associate with the Blurock Partnership in 1989, Russell opened his own practice. Russell is LEED accredited and guides the design studio on environmentally sensitive design technology and knowledge.

ROBIN DONALDSON AIA, was born in Pasadena, CA, in 1957, and received a BA in Studio Art and Art History at the University of California at Santa Barbara. In 1986, he received his Master of Architecture, at Southern California Institute of Architecture (SCI-Arc). While a student at SCI-Arc, Donaldson began working with the renowned Morphosis studio, assuming project architect responsibilities on commercial, institutional, and residential projects. In 1990, Donaldson founded Shubin + Donaldson Architects (S+D) with Russell Shubin.

Practicing architecture is a challenging but rewarding profession. There are times in the trenches with bullets whizzing over our heads, where were it not for the support of a full regiment of committed architects and staff, none of the projects in this book would have been realized. We know that working at S+D is not all glory, riches and fame. Yet all of the survivors of the S+D boot camp, have hopefully gained a deeper understanding of the commitment, integrity, and passion it takes to get even a half-way decent project built. It is our honor and profound satisfaction to dedicate this book to all of you.

Of the many great architects, assistants and staff that have been part of the team over the last 20 years, Mark Hershman has grown to be a true partner with Russell in the Los Angeles office. He stood by Russell's side and shouldered a significant share of the design and management in the execution of key projects in this book and has been a true partner in the fortunes of S+D.

Our Partnership has been strengthened by the support and coaching of Patricia McDade, Barry Pogorel, Hugh Hochberg, Julie Taylor, and Ralph White.

This book is also dedicated to our clients. Without them, there would be no cause for a book such as this. We would like to thank all of the clients who made the choice to work with us. We consider it an honor to assume the responsibility that clients bestow upon us to make their dreams and goals become built reality. This book is a narrow but representative survey of the hundreds of projects we have completed over the past 20 years. In particular we would like to acknowledge Seth and Monica Epstein, Jim Smith and Court Crandall, Ann and Bob Diener, Alvin and Nancy Whitehead, Genie Gable and Geoffrey Moore, John and Debbie Warfel, Mike and Laurie Nathan, Colin and Greg Strause, David Angelo, Noam Murro, Jonathan Notaro, Ben and Monica Weiner, Scott Painter, and Marcia and John Mike Cohen.

ACKNOWLEDGEMENTS

RUSSELL SHUBIN

In the fall of 1980, at a particularly fortunate time, I was accepted to Cal Poly San Luis Obispo amongst a group of talented, inquisitive individuals. Looking back on my formal education and the early professional years that followed, it was these individuals that had been the catalysts for the conversations that would inform my thinking, and ultimately clarify my design point of view. I would like to acknowledge this talented, impactful group: Mark Macy, Dennis Hollingsworth, Troy Sizemore, Daniel Piechota, David Winslow, Maya Shimoguchi, Michael Lusso, Tim Power, Leo Marmol, Ron Radziner, Lorcan O'Herlihy, Ric Abramson, Jim Brown, Jim Gates, and Robin Brisebois, I thank you.

Also, I acknowledge Robin for his simple God-given talent and vision, and his fortitude in observing and harnessing the various individual strengths of the staff that have worked with us over the years. For seeing all people for who they can be, rather than for what they are not. Thank you for always supporting me over the past 20 years no matter what the circumstances.

I want to thank my parents Jo Ann and Johnny for always championing me and understanding the time commitment that my work has taken over the years. Thank you to our publicist Julie Taylor who has been our most resilient advocate, with us since the very beginning. I also want to thank my dear friends Jerome Downes, Michael Lusso, Jan Horn, and Seth Epstein for their illuminating conversations, loyalty, and advocacy of our practice. I want to acknowledge Ken La Spada and Cary Gerhardt, of Sierra Pacific Constructors, for their willingness to continually jump through any hoops we requested to insure each of our interior's projects leveraged our particular point of view.

Finally, I want to thank my wife and partner Erica for continually encouraging me to do what I have needed to do in order to grow our practice over the years; for her uncanny ability to be both a force in the business world, and a loving, nurturing mother to our sons.

To my two spirited sons, Brach and Quaid, thank you for providing so much joy and inspiring me each day to get out there and do it!

ROBIN DONALDSON

This book is about buildings, but it's an extraordinary circle of people that for me are the real story.

In the fall of 1983, thanks to the suggestion of my UCSB Architectural History Professor David Gebhard, I crossed the threshold of a ramshackle Santa Monica warehouse housing the Southern California Institute of Architecture (SCI-Arc). Thus unveiled a crackling untethered new world of architectural thinking and possibilities presided over by SCI-Arc founder Ray Kappe. Like an architectural Dumbledore, he presided over burgeoning architectural wizards such as Eric Moss, Robert Mangurian, Michael Rotondi, and Thom Mayne. I was fortunate to enjoy the educational benefit of rubbing elbows with this rare confluence of architectural masters and the richness of this experience was enhanced all the more by my immediate recruitment into the emerging studio of Morphosis. I can only hope that the work in this book does not embarrass this extraordinary group of mentors.

Also, I acknowledge Russell. His perseverance, integrity, and indomitable spirit carried me through many rocky stretches. Thank you for sharing the ups and downs of 20 years of partnership in a tough but ultimately soul-satisfying sport. Thank you for "getting who I am..." and thank you for your respect.

Thank you to Heather Peterson for working with me on this book and doing her best to keep me on track philosophically. A particular thank you to Thom Mayne whose stardom has never surprised me, but who's extraordinary availability, generosity, and guidance for young architects has. Special thanks to Bill and Joan Crawford, Paul Franz, Paul Tuttle (in memoriam), Kurt Helfrich, Fred Hill, Seth Epstein, Alan Axelrod, Brett Ettinger, and Pam Ferguson for your friendship, insight, laughter, and select perspective on what I've been doing for the last 20 years. To my brothers Mark and David, you guys are creative geniuses and have given me a context for pursuing my art. Thanks to my parents Bob and Sherry who would slow down as we drove by the first building my young eyes ever admired, the Los Angeles City Hall.

Finally, I don't know where I would be or what my life would be like without Eryn. Your trust, support and partnership illuminates my daily world. Thank you.

To my beautiful young sons Reed and Payne, rock on!

HONORS AND AWARDS

AIA/LA Decade Merit Award, 2005 (Ground Zero)
AIA/LA Interior Architecture Merit Award, 2001
(Ogilvy & Mather)
FX International Interior Design Awards Finalist, 2001
(Ogilvy & Mather)
FX International Interior Design Awards Finalist, 2001
(Ground Zero)
Business Week/Architectural Record Awards Winner, 2000
(Ground Zero)
AIA/LA Interior Architecture Honor Award, 2000 (Mindfield)
AIA/LA Interior Architecture Honorable Mention, 2000
(Iwin.com)
Interiors Magazine Design Award Honorable Mention, 2000
(Iwin.com)
2000 Lumen West Award of Merit (Ground Zero)
Business Week/Architectural Record Awards Finalist, 1999
(Ground Zero)
AIA/LA Interior Architecture Honor Award, 1999 (Ground Zero)
Next/AIA/LA Award, 1999 (Mindfield)
Next/AIA/LA Award, 1999 (Santa Monica Sound Studio)
"New Faces," Contract Design Magazine, 1999
(Shubin + Donaldson)
California Council/AIA Design Award, 1998
(Fuel Design and Production)
AIA/Santa Barbara Award, 1998 (Trout Club Residence)
AIA/Santa Barbara Award, 1998
(LA County Sheriff's Youth Center)
AIA/Santa Barbara Chapter President, 1998
(Robin Donaldson)
Laguna Beach AIA Merit Award, 1995 (Urban Residence)
40 Under 40, 1995 (Robin Donaldson)

PUBLICATIONS

NEWSPAPERS + PERIODICALS

Santa Barbara Homeowner; "Art by the Sea" (Cover); July 2008
Home by Design; "Waterfront Living: Summer Is About Simple Pleasures"; June/July 2008
Interior Design Magazine; "The Hybrid"; May 2008
Santa Barbara Homeowner; "Modern Riviera" (Cover); May 2008
Contract Design Magazine; "Practice: Tiny Dancers"; March 2008
Custom Home Magazine; "Outer Limits: Art of the Matter"; March 2008
Angeleno Magazine; "The Radar Design: Form Meets Faction"; March 2008
The Robb Report Collection; "Building Blocks"; March 2008
Lodging Hospitality Magazine; "HOT Confab Tinting Greener"; February 2008
Hospitality Design Magazine: The Source 2008; "Design/Architectural Firms"; 2008

Angeleno Magazine; "Second-Home Run!"; December 2007
Hinge (Hong Kong); "Home Coming...New Domestic Architecture From All Over"; December 2007
Multi-Housing News; "Green Design + Conference and Expo"; December 2007
Hospitality Construction; "Industry Events"; November/December 2007
California Construction; "Top Design Firms in America"; October 2007
Interior Design Magazine; "Howdy Doody"; October 2007
MARU Interior Design (Korea); "Interiors II" (Cover); October 2007
ArcCA; "This Century So Far: a Sketch of the AIACC Design Awards"; 3rd quarter 2007
Dwell Design Source; "Architects and Designers"; July/August 2007
Alaska Airlines; "Real Estate: Hobby Havens—Home Is Where the Art Is"; July 2007
Horizon Air; "Real Estate: Hobby Havens—Home Is Where the Art Is"; July 2007
O at Home; "Calvin Klein Home ad"; Summer 2007
Domino; "Calvin Klein Home ad"; May 2007
Elle Décor; "Calvin Klein Home ad"; May 2007
Metropolitan Home; "Calvin Klein Home ad"; May 2007
House & Garden; "Calvin Klein Home ad"; April 2007
Hospitality Construction; "Green Centerpiece to Highlight Green Products in Hospitality Setting"; March/April 2007
LA Architect; "New Design: Enterprise"; March/April 2007
The New York Times Style Magazine; "Calvin Klein Home ad"; Spring 2007
Hospitality Construction; "Special Report: Top Hospitality Architecture Firms"; January/February 2007
LA Architect; "New Design"; January/February 2007
Kitchen Trends; "A Whole Range of Possibilities"; 2007

California Construction; "2006 Top Architecture Firms in California"; October 2006
LA Architect; "AIA Decade Award/Merit"; October 2006
Los Angeles Business Journal; "People: Kudos"; August 14, 2006
Luxury Spa Finder; "Dream Home Spa: Space Craft"; July/August 2006
AIA/LA 2006 Design Awards Program; "Decade Awards: Merit Awards"; June 8, 2006
Urban Land; "Proactive Solution File: California's Creative-Class Warehouse Offices"; March 2006
Trends Very Best Kitchens & Bathrooms; "Command Post"; Spring 2006
Interior Design Magazine; "Church Of The Open Mind"; February 2006
Interior Design Magazine; "Newsdesk: Blue And Green"; February 2006
Dream Baths Magazine; "Beauty Spots: Vacation Inspiration"; 2006

Dwell; "Dwell Design Guide: Architects and Designers"; October/November 2005
Contract Design Magazine; "Focus: Made To Order"; June 2005
Contract Design Magazine; "Design: Add Campaign"; June 2005
LA Architect; "Site Profile"; May/June 2005
Archidom (Russia); "Hi-Tech Production"; April 2005
LA Architect; "Work Spaces"; November/December 2005
Kitchen Trends; "Command Post"; Volume 21/3 2005

Los Angeles Times Magazine; "Style/Home: Latin Accents"; November 28, 2004
Real Estate Southern California; "Guide To Suppliers: Architecture/Design/Engineering"; June 2004
Colorfulness (China); "Waterfront House: On Golden Sand"; June 2004
Better Homes & Gardens Beautiful Baths; "Souvenir Palette"; November 2004
Robb Report; "2004 Ultimate Home Tour: A Great Estate—The Façade" (Cover); April 2004
Los Angeles Times Magazine; "The Kitchen Maximized"; February 8, 2004

California Home & Design; "Winners of the 4th Annual CH&D Design Achievement Awards" (Cover); October 2003
Kitchen Trends; "Light Refreshment"; Volume 19/5 2003
Los Angeles Times Magazine; "Lighting: Glass Menagerie"; September 28, 2003
Interior Design Magazine; "The Firm's Firm"; May 2003

Metropolitan Home; "Sand Box"; March/April, 2003
People Magazine; "On the Block: Hollywood by the Sea"; January 20, 2003
Bathroom Trends; "Get Comfortable—Lounge Space"; Volume 19/3 2003
SAH/SCC News; "Featured Event: Architectural Tour with Shubin + Donaldson"; January/February 2003

Los Angeles Times Magazine; "Not Your Father's Office" (Cover); September 29, 2002
Frame (The Netherlands); "The Dixie Chicks Were Here"; September/October 2002
Angeleno Magazine; "Warming Trend: A Modern House Finds A Home In Montecito"; September/October 2002
Riviera; "Warming Trend: A Modern House Finds A Home In Montecito"; September/October 2002
Chicago Social; "Warming Trend: A Modern House Finds A Home In Montecito"; September 2002
Los Angeles Magazine; "Good Bones: A Solid Foundation For A Spectacular Renovation"; September 2002
LA Architect; "The Power Of Light"; July/August 2002
LA Architect; "Photo Album: The Firm"; July/August 2002
Interior Design; "Modern in Montecito"; June 2002
Architectural Record; "Small; Medium; and Large: Lessons From the Best-Managed Firms; Part II"; June 2002
Contract; "Fitting In: Fotouhi Alonso Associates"; June 2002
Architectural Record; "Small; Medium; and Large: Lessons From the Best-Managed Firms"; May 2002
LA Architect; "Profile—dTank: A New Tradition of the Work Space"; Mar/Apr 2002
Blueprint (United Kingdom); "News: Interiors—Tunnel Visions"; February 2002
LA Architect; "AIA/LA 2001 Awards"; January/February 2002

Interior Design: The Best of 2001; "Best Office: Ogilvy & Mather"; December 2001
AMC (France); "Interieurs—Shubin & Donaldson Architects Bureaux Mixtes Los Angeles"; December 2001
Frame (The Netherlands); "Items: Workstation"; November/December 2001
California Real Estate Journal; "Architecture: AIA/LA Honors 23 Design Projects"; November 5, 2001
LA Architect; "Upfront: Awards"; November/December 2001
Contract Design Magazine; "Focus: New Customs"; November 2001
LA Architect; "Shedding the 'Blue Suit'"; September/October 2001
Los Angeles Business Journal; "Corporate Expansion & Relocation—Ogilvy Makes Its Move"; August 27-September 2, 2001
Frame (The Netherlands); "Workplace Issue: Tube Station"; July/August 2001
Interiors; "It's On The Prize"; June 2001

ArchitecturalRecord.com; "Themes of Transparency are Grounded by Raw Design Elements"; June 2001
OFX (Italy); "Interiors: The Headquarters of Advertising Agency 'Ground Zero' is the Best Visiting Card"; March/April 2001
Interior Design; "Tunnel Vision" (Cover); March 2001
Tasarim (Turkey); "Office Buildings: Fotouhi Alonso Associates; California"; #109 (2001)
Tasarim (Turkey); "Office Buildings: LRN-Network"; #109 (2001)
Contract; "Branching Out"; March 2001
FX (Italy); "Lofty Ideals"; January 2001
Revolution; "Online Media: Iwin.com"; January 2001

Business Week International (European Ed.); "Business Week/Architectural Record Awards—Super Structures: Frugal, But Full of Energy and Light"; November 6, 2000
Business Week; "Frugal, But Full of Energy and Light"; November 6, 2000
LA Architect; "2000 AIA/LA Awards"; November/December 2000
OFX Special Office International (Italy); "A Radical Transformation"; Nov/ Dec 2000
Time; "My Kingdom for a Door"; October 23, 2000
Architectural Record; "Theatrical Architecture Nourishes Ad Agency Ideas"; Oct 2000
AIArchitect; "Business Week/Architectural Record Award Winners"; October 2000
Interiors; "5 Years Ago in Interiors"; September 2000
American HomeStyle & Gardening: Kitchen & Bath Custom Planner; "The Wild Blue Yonder" (Cover); Fall 2000
Los Angeles Business Journal; What are Top-Flight Los Angeles Executives Looking for in Their Offices?"; August 7–13, 2000
LA Architect; "LA Architect Launches at Ground Zero"; May/June 2000
LA Architect; "Awards"; September/October 2000
Architectural Record; "A California Firm Revels in Digital Age"; March 2000
LA Architect; "Honor Awards: Ground Zero"; January/February 2000

The Architectural Review (United Kingdom); "Billboard Building"; October 1999
Interiors; "Point of Impact" (Cover); October 1999
Los Angeles Business Journal; "Creativity by Design"; September 20, 1999
Graphis; "The Glory of Raw Space"; July/August 1999
The New York Times; "Now Playing in Los Angeles: Have Warehouse; Will Remodel"; May 13, 1999
Contract Design Magazine; "Where There's Fuel There's Fire" (Cover); January 1999
Los Angeles Business Journal; "Lost in the Funhouse at Ground Zeroland"; January 11–17, 1999

Los Angeles Times Orange County; "Bravura New World"; January 9, 1999

SCI-Arc Alumni News; "Shubin + Donaldson Win Award"; Summer 1998
Daily Variety; "Wild Workplaces: Fuel's Idea Factory"; July 31, 1998
Los Angeles Times; "Architecture Review: Bravura New World"; April 18, 1998
Los Angeles Times; "Commercial Real Estate: A Loft of Fun"; March 10, 1998
The New York Times; "Crime-Fighting Design"; February 19, 1998
Architectural Record; "A Gang-Proof Youth Center"; February 1998

LA Architect; "Six Emerging Architects"; August/September 1997
Architectural Digest; "Seaside Simplicity in Malibu"; April 1997

The New York Times Magazine; "Monumental Minimalism"; February 25, 1996

Interiors; "40 Under 40"; September 1995

BOOKS

Ecological Architecture; Braun, Germany; 2009
M2 360° Interior Design II; Sandu Publishing, China; 2009
M3 360° Modern Architecture II; Sandu Publishing, China; 2009
Pool Design; Daab, Germany; 2008
The New 100 Houses x 100 Architects; Images Publishing Group, Australia; 2007
American Spaces; Images Publishing Group, Australia; 2007
Interior Architecture Now; Laurence King Publishing, UK; 2007
Residential Designs for the 21st Century: An International Collection; Firefly Books, USA; 2007
25 Espaces de Bureaux; Amc LeMoniteur, France; 2006
25 Houses Under 3000 Square Feet; Collins Design, USA; 2006
2000 Architects; Images Publishing Group, Australia; 2006
Beach Houses; Feierabend Verlag, Germany; 2006
Outdoor Rooms II; Quarry Books, USA; 2006
A Pocketful of Houses; Images Publishing Group, Australia; 2006
The Contemporary Guesthouse; Edizioni Press, USA; 2005
Pacific Houses; Harper Design International, USA; 2004
Offices Design Source (Cover); Harper Collins, USA; 2004
Interiors Now; Images Publishing Group, Australia; 2004
34 Los Angeles Architects; A+D Museum, USA; 2004
50+ Great Bathrooms By Architects; Images Publishing Group, Australia; 2005
50 Great Kitchens By Architects; Images Publishing Group, Australia; 2005
100 More Of The World's Best Houses; Images Publishing Group, Australia; 2005
Kids Spaces; Images Publishing Group, Australia; 2004
Pacific Houses; Harper Design International, USA; 2004
The Other Office: Creative Workplace Design; Frame: Birkhauser, The Netherlands; 2004
1000 Architects; Images Publishing Group, Australia; 2004
The 21st Century Office; Laurence King Publishing, UK; 2003
Another 100 Of The World's Best Houses; Images Publishing Group, Australia; 2003
New Offices; Loft Publications, Spain; August 2003
Offices: Designer & Design; Loft Publications, Spain; 2003
Office Spaces: Volume 1; Images Publishing Group, Australia, 2003
100 Of The World's Best Houses; Images Publishing Group, Australia; 2002
Interior Spaces of The USA and Canada; Volume 6 (Cover); Images Publishing Group, Australia; 2002
Workspheres; The Museum of Modern Art, USA; 2001
Details in Architecture; Volume 3; Images Publishing Group, Australia; 2001
International Architecture Yearbook; Volume 7; Images Publishing Group, Australia; 2001
Cyberspace: The World of Digital Architecture; Images Publishing Group, Australia; 2000
Architecture + Design LA; The Understanding Business Press, USA; 2000
Los Angeles Home Book; (First Edition); Cahners Publishing, USA; 2000
Shops & Boutiques 2000; PBC International, USA; 2000
Outdoor Rooms; Rockport Publishers, USA; 1999
The Creative Office; Calmann & King, UK; 1999
Building in Los Angeles; Southern California Institute of Architecture, USA; 1999
Designing With Spirituality; PBC International, USA; 1999
Interiorscapes: Design Ideas for Rooms With a View; Rockport Publishers, USA; 1999
Room by Room: Contemporary Interior; Rockport Publishers, USA; 1999
Amazing Space: Architect Designed Homes Under $300,000; Schiffer Publishing, USA; 1998
Building in Los Angeles; Southern California Institute of Architecture, USA; 1998
40 Under 40: A Guide to New Young Talent; Vitae Press, USA; 1995

CONTACT INFO

SHUBIN + DONALDSON ARCHITECTS INC.

LOS ANGELES OFFICE

3834 WILLAT AVENUE
CULVER CITY, CA 90232
T. 310.204.0688

SANTA BARBARA OFFICE

1 NORTH CALLE CESAR CHAVEZ, SUITE 200
SANTA BARBARA, CA 93103
T. 805.966.2802

contact@sandarc.com
www.shubinanddonaldson.com

PHOTOGRAPHY CREDITS

FARSHID ASSASSI 140-149 / 200 **TOM BONNER** COVER / 3-5 / 8-13 / 18-31 / 38-59 / 120-139 / 158-171 / 184-189 / 201-202 / 224 / 234-235 **CIRO COELHO** COVER / 2 / 32-37 / 60-79 / 90-119 / 150-157 / 172-183 / 205 / 215 / 219 / 246 / 252 **JIMMY COHRSSEN** 6-7 / 14-15

BOOK DESIGN

ART DIRECTION / DESIGN ROBIN DONALDSON AIA **GRAPHIC DESIGN** HEATHER PETERSON **BOOK PRODUCTION** HEATHER PETERSON / JULIE TAYLOR **COPY EDITS** HEATHER PETERSON / JULIE TAYLOR **PLANS AND DIAGRAMS** ANDREW JOHNSTON / HEATHER PETERSON / JANG HEE YOO